RUTH CULHAM

Dream Wakers

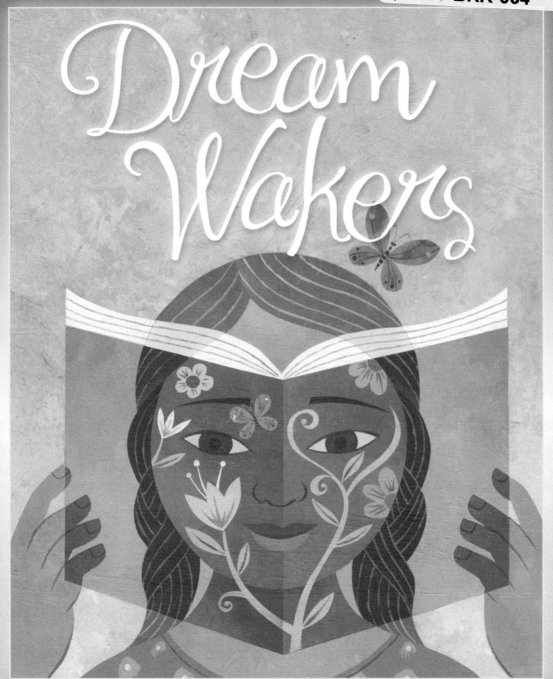

MENTOR TEXTS THAT CELEBRATE LATINO CULTURE

foreword by PAM MUÑOZ RYAN

 Stenhouse Publishers
Portland, Maine

Stenhouse Publishers
www.stenhouse.com

Library of Congress Cataloging-in-Publication Data
Names: Culham, Ruth, author.
Title: Dream wakers : mentor texts that celebrate Latino culture /
    Ruth Culham.
Description: Portland, Maine : Stenhouse Publishers, 2016. | Includes
    bibliographical references.
Identifiers: LCCN 2016018739 (print) | LCCN 2016032203 (ebook) |
    ISBN 9781625311115 (pbk. : alk. paper) | ISBN 9781625311122
    (ebook) Subjects: LCSH: English language—Composition and
    exercises—Study and teaching (Elementary) | Composition
    (Language arts)—Study and teaching (Elementary) | Children's
    literature—Study and teaching (Elementary) | Hispanic Americans—
    Study and teaching (Elementary) | Hispanic Americans in literature.
Classification: LCC LB1576 .C8464 2016 (print) | LCC LB1576 (ebook)
    | DDC 372.62/3—dc23
LC record available at https://lccn.loc.gov/2016018739

Cover illustration by Rafael López; cover design by Beth Ford; interior design and typesetting by Martha Drury

Manufactured in the United States of America

PRINTED ON 30% PCW
RECYCLED PAPER

22 21 20 19 18 17   9 8 7 6 5 4 3 2

To Sam, always,
and to Ray, for always believing

✿ CONTENTS ✿

Foreword by Pam Muñoz Ryan   vii

Acknowledgments   ix

Chapter 1   WORDS TO AWAKEN DREAMS: THE IMPORTANCE
            OF MENTOR TEXTS THAT CELEBRATE LATINO CULTURE   1

Chapter 2   THE CENTER OF ATTENTION: IDEAS   21

Chapter 3   THE METICULOUS PLANNER: ORGANIZATION   43

Chapter 4   THE ENERGIZER: VOICE   63

Chapter 5   THE NITPICKER: WORD CHOICE   81

Chapter 6   THE CONVERSATIONALIST: SENTENCE FLUENCY   101

Chapter 7   THE CURMUDGEON: CONVENTIONS   123

Epilogue   DREAM WAKERS: FINAL THOUGHTS   137

            Appendix A: The Book Selection Process   139

            Appendix B: Books and Traits at a Glance   143

            Professional References Cited   161

 FOREWORD

Dear Educators,

My earliest memory of reading was at my Mexican grandmother's house. She lived a few blocks away, so I spent much of my after-school and free time there. In her living room, on the bottom shelf of a bookcase, was an entire set of encyclopedias. I'm not sure how they came to be there or how she could afford them. No one in my neighborhood had such a thing. She was a fan of buying things from door-to-door salesmen—an enormous juicer, a vacuum, cosmetics—so I suspect some fast-talker persuaded her to buy the set over time. I was fascinated by the encyclopedias and spent hours flipping through the pages and "reading" before I could ever decipher a sentence.

Even though my kindergarten class picture looks like an ad for the United Nations, that diversity was not reflected in the print I saw at school. Curriculum was different then, in Bakersfield, California, in the late 1950s. I learned to read from primers and, later, from a thick reading book with dictated content. There were no trade books in the classroom, and there was no diverting from the prescribed text. This was years before the idea of multiculturalism came to education.

I didn't discover the library until fifth grade. We had moved across town, and I was the new kid on the block and the new kid at a school where everyone had been together for years. I did not fit in. I started riding my bike to the small branch library near my house and filling my bike basket with books, repeating the journey every weekend. That memory is so vivid that even today I can relive the exact route I took down the alley, through the Knights of Columbus property, over a bumpy dirt field, into the parking lot of Green Frog Market, and down Bernard Street to the Baker Street library.

Like the route to the library that is etched into my memory, those books of my young adolescence are carved into my soul: *Treasure Island, The Swiss Family Robinson, Anne of Green Gables, Little Women*, and the Sue Barton, Nurse series. If I loved a book, I didn't read it just once. I read it many times. The act of reading and escaping into books allowed me to live many more lives than my real one. Books helped me cope during a time of my life when I was struggling socially. I was comforted by the characters' lives as I muddled through my own.

I'm going to be honest. As a young child, I never once wondered why I didn't see myself or my family in books. I'm not sure why. Like many children, I went to school, obedient and unquestioning. And even though I had a rich experience with books outside of school, I did not realize that some people were not represented, that some people were marginalized. Once I entered college, though, and began a career in education, I began to wonder how different my reading experience might have been if I had read *just one book* with which I could identify.

Just one.

Today, I have had that experience, through the back door. My book *Esperanza Rising* has been in print since 2001. I have received thousands of letters from many Latino children and adults about what the story has meant to them and their families. I have felt their sense of ownership and pride, vicariously, when they've told me I was writing *for them*. I am filled with joy when readers tell me that I wrote *their story*. That said, *as important* to me are the letters I have received from non-Latino children and adults of all ethnicities who tell me what the book meant to them. One boy wrote to me, "I didn't know about those things in your book, until you told them to my eyes."

We no longer live pedestrian lives. We live in a world that is made larger by television, the Internet, print media, and the accessibility of travel. We are preparing children to meet not only their neighborhood, but a much broader existence, filled with people from all walks of life, who speak many languages, whose families originated from many different countries.

We can't just look at people—at their countenances, their clothing, or the color of their skin—and understand them. We have to first hear a person's *story*. And readers need more than one story. They need a smorgasbord of stories about families and cultures, traditions and holidays, histories and realities. Reading a breadth of stories nurtures the seeds of understanding.

No matter the length of the strides that have been made, I'm proud of and amazed by how far education has come since I was in elementary school. And I'm hopeful about the future of students' reading experiences. That is why this book is an important resource: With its wealth of direction and titles, *Dream Wakers* will help teachers and readers open their eyes a little wider.

Pam Muñoz Ryan

☸ ACKNOWLEDGMENTS ☸

The inspiration for this book came from teachers several years ago at Colorado Council International Reading Association in Denver. After I had shared mentor texts with a workshop group, several teachers asked, "Do you have anything like this for our Latino students?" I didn't. And even worse, I didn't even have a cache of titles to offer them as a starter kit. I knew that had to change.

This began my love affair with Latino children's literature. I began ordering books and reading and reading and reading. I used award lists to start and then the Amazon.com recommendations "Customers Who Bought This Item Also Bought . . ." and my collection grew and grew. These books evoked warm, loving, and exhilarating emotions. And some broke my heart with their poignancy.

I wondered how my writing about these books might be received. After all, I am not Latino. I am white. I asked Latino educators across the country what they thought and was gratified by their responses. One group in Miami said that the issue was quality, not race. They respected my ability to select high-quality children's books and write about them so teachers could use them with integrity in their teaching. Thank you for that vote of confidence. And teachers across the country reminded me of another good point: *Dream Wakers* is just as much about broadening *everyone's* collection and understanding of Latino children's literature as it is about teaching Latino students. One of the goals of this book is for all students to learn about this dazzling culture. So I began writing.

Imagine my joy when renowned children's authors began to say "yes!" when I asked them to share their insights in original essays for this book. They wrote heartfelt pieces about their experiences, motivations, and writing processes. You know how it feels the first time you hike to the top of a mountain and look down at the valley below—that sense of awe and wonder? That's how I felt when essays from Alma Flor Ada, F. Isabel Campoy, Yuyi Morales, Duncan Tonatiuh, Margarita Engle, Enrique Flores-Galbis, Monica Brown, Susan Middleton Elya, Joe Hayes, and Jeanette Winter came pouring in. Then Rafael López—the magnificent artist whose work I've admired for years—agreed without hesitation to create original art for the cover; Pam Muñoz Ryan, my friend and colleague, wrote the fore-word that gave me goose bumps and happy tears. My heart soars! Thank you all for your beautiful words and art, your work, and your faith in this book. I'm humbled by your generosity.

No book is written solely by the author, however. There is at least one other person who is integral to bringing it to life: the editor. Tori Bachman, Stenhouse wonder-editor, thank you for every single phone call, e-mail, text, edit, question, probe, note, laugh, and insight throughout the evolution of this book, from manuscript notes through final pages. Draft after draft, you believed in the promise of the book and the author. There are no words to express how grateful I am to you, to Louisa Irele, and to everyone else at Stenhouse for this opportunity.

Chapter 1

WORDS TO AWAKEN DREAMS

THE IMPORTANCE OF MENTOR TEXTS THAT CELEBRATE LATINO CULTURE

When I was a young girl, I spent my days reading. I admit it—I was a book geek even then. My happiest time was going to the public library where the very forward-thinking librarian recognized a voracious reader when she saw one and waived the two-book-a-week limit.

The books with which I connected the most strongly were written so well that I fell into them, imagining myself as the protagonist. I became Dorothy Gale by standing by the grandfather clock in the hallway of my grandparents' house at one o'clock on Saturdays, clicking my heels together, opening the book, and being transported to Oz. I lived with Laura Ingalls Wilder by inhaling page after page, book after book, while imagining that I, too, had a loving yet unbearably hard life on the prairie—in much simpler times. I experienced life on a farm through Fern Arable, and I laughed and wept. As I read E. B. White's transformative book, I felt as though I was the one rescuing Wilbur.

I grew up in Los Angeles, so imagine how foreign Oz, the Midwest prairie, and a farm were to me. I grew as a reader and thinker by reading those books and many others. I developed my moral compass because of these books. My sense of compassion blossomed with each reading, and I learned what it meant to be a person with integrity even in the face of life's most difficult challenges.

If we are lucky, every one of us has important books that shaped our early views of the world and all of its possibilities. But here's what I've come to realize: No matter how breathtaking the books or how foreign their settings and captivating their stories, all my favorite books as a child had white, female protagonists. At many levels, I related to them because I, too, am white and female. Their pages spoke to me, the young reader, and fueled my love of language, which burns to this very day. What I've learned as an adult is the importance of reading books by a range of authors who write in many genres, fiction and nonfiction, that I never explored as a younger reader. Now I actively seek voices from a full spectrum of authors—women and men from a variety of cultural backgrounds—to gain multiple perspectives and to experience the world in ways I never could through my own eyes. Here is the big question, though: Would I have developed the same yearning for words and literature, developed a passion for lifelong reading, if I had not seen myself reflected in those early books?

In *The Importance of Diversity in Library Programs and Material Collections for Children* (Naidoo 2014), we discover two important reasons for placing diverse texts in the hands of students as early as possible: (1) to help children identify with characters, settings, and pieces of information that are culturally relevant to them, and (2) to expand their view of the world and the people and societies in it. Naidoo expresses concern that there be an emphasis on making sure there are positive representations of diversity in children's materials to

- *provide positive role models for culturally diverse children;*
- *introduce children to characters with similar experiences and emotions;*
- *convey the richness and beauty of the diverse cultures in the United States;*
- *reinforce a distinct cultural identity;*
- *promote multilingual and literacy development;*
- *inspire learning of other cultures and general cultural knowledge;*
- *facilitate acceptance of cultures different from one's own; and*
- *foster global connections.* (6)

The report goes on to explain in great detail the sociocultural psychology research of Vygotsky (1986), Bishop (1997), Hughes-Hassell and

Cox (2010), and others, and the effect on children's self-image of meeting people like themselves in what they read. You'll notice, too, in the preceding list how reading diverse children's books in school can influence the social and identity development of *all* students in a classroom, regardless of skin color or cultural background. Diverse texts help us understand ourselves, our neighbors, our society, our world.

No wonder I blossomed as a reader when I was young. The texts I read met that standard, enabling me to develop as a person as well as a reader. Lucky me. However, many of the children we serve in today's schools do not have access to texts that reflect who they are, how they look, or what their home culture is like. I highly recommend reading the Naidoo report in its entirety, along with other reports, articles, and books in the reference list at the end of this book. We must make sure students of all backgrounds have access to high-quality, culturally diverse texts and recognize the difference those texts will make in their reading lives as well as in their perception of themselves as thinkers, learners, and citizens.

Now consider this: according to the National Center for Information in the *Profile of Teachers in the U.S. 2011*, 84 percent of teachers are female; 84 percent of teachers are white (Feinstritzer 2011). However, according to an article by Lesli A. Maxwell (2014) in *Education Week*, "The new collective majority of minority schoolchildren—projected to be 50.3 percent by the National Center for Education Statistics—is driven largely by dramatic growth in the Latino population and a decline in the white population, and, to a lesser degree, by a steady rise in the number of Asian-Americans. African-American growth has been mostly flat" (1).

The moral imperative of those of us who are white educators, then, is to search high and low for high-quality reading materials that feature cultural diversity. Not always easy, when we consider findings of a more recent study from the University of Wisconsin, reflected in Figure 1.1: Only 3.3 percent of children's books published are by and about Hispanic culture, and only 1.3 percent reflect African American culture (Cooperative Children's Book Center 2014). These publication numbers may vary slightly because of the CCBC's deadlines for submitting books, but the trend is obvious: the numbers of children's books being published that represent diverse cultures are pitifully small, making them hard to find. But seek diverse books we must, because our students—all of our students—need them. Consider this poem by Alma Flor Ada, which I discovered in the foreword of *Multicultural Literature for Latino Bilingual Children* (Clark et al. 2016), then close your eyes and visualize the faces in your classroom:

Books let me fly,
they let me soar.
Books open windows
and magic doors.
Sometimes they whisper,
sometimes they roar.

Sometimes I find
someone who looks like me,
feels like me,
thinks like me.

Sometimes I find more of who I want to be.

Books let me fly,
they let me soar.
They open windows
and magic doors.

Sometimes they whisper,
sometimes they roar. (ix)

For the reasons many prominent researchers and educators have put forth, and for reasons relating to my own experience and sense of urgency, I've come to believe that putting the right book at the right time in the hands of a child is a critical mission of every literacy teacher. According to the NPR interview with First Book CEO Kyle Zimmer, "New Initiative Aims to Encourage Diversity in Kids' Publishing," "[W]hen kids see themselves in books, they are far more likely to become enthusiastic readers. But we also know that this isn't just about seeing themselves in books, this is also about kids seeing other kids in books, and other cultures in books" (Neary 2014, 2).

The goal for providing diverse books, then, is twofold: (1) self-reflection and (2) appreciation of cultures other than one's own. Maya Christina Gonzalez (2015) notes the following:

> When children don't see themselves reflected in their book, a common
> experience for most Latino children, they are being told in one of the
> most effective and powerful ways that their experience is not valuable,
> and by extension, neither are they. This does not make for a positive
> learning environment inside or outside the classroom or support the
> development of personal worth within the larger context of society. (2)

Figure 1.1 Children's Books By and About People of Color and First/Native Nations Published in the United States, 2002–2014

Year	Total Number of Books Published (Est.)	Number of Books Received at CCBC	African/ African Americans		American Indians		Asian Pacifics/ Asian Pacific Americans		Latinos	
			By	About	By	About	By	About	By	About
2014	5,000	3,500	84	180	20	38	129	112	59	66
2013	5,000	3,200	68	93	18	34	90	69	48	57
2012	5,000	3,600	68	119	6	22	83	76	59	54
2011	5,000	3,400	79	123	12	28	76	91	52	58
2010	5,000	3,400	102	156	9	22	60	64	55	66
2009	5,000	3,000	83	157	12	33	67	80	60	61
2008	5,000	3,000	83	172	9	40	77	98	48	79
2007	5,000	3,000	77	150	6	44	56	68	42	59
2006	5,000	3,000	87	153	14	41	72	74	42	63
2005	5,000	2,800	75	149	4	34	60	64	50	76
2004	5,000	2,800	99	143	7	33	61	65	37	61
2003	5,000	3,200	79	171	11	95	43	78	41	63
2002	5,000	3,150	69	166	6	64	46	91	48	94

Source: Cooperative Children's Book Center 2014

This is an important point: if we grow up in a world where the great thinkers and characters in the literature we read, the characters in movies and TV shows we watch, and the people with whom we spend time all look like us, how do we develop a sense of the world outside our neighborhoods? It's through a rich, technicolored collection of print and nonprint media that reflect the values and strengths of *every* culture that we learn about and come to understand provinces beyond our own.

Dr. Judi Moreillon of Texas Women's University reinforces this thinking: "An excellent way to build cultural bridges is to integrate authentic contemporary children's literature about diverse groups into library programs to promote cultural literacy and global understanding, thereby introducing children to the rich cultures of their peers, teachers, or future acquaintances" (Naidoo 2014, 5). And esteemed children's author

Pat Mora (2016) comments, "We live in a diverse country with cultural riches. Latino children, and all our children, deserve to see their lives in the pages of the books they read. Books convey powerful messages about what—and who—matters" (12).

It's not only traditional reading that helps us continue to grow and expand thinking; there are examples of digital media that bring the issue of culture into focus as well. While researching titles for this book, I found an eloquent video, a short and powerful piece by Alma Flor Ada, one of my writing heroes, and her son Gabriel M. Zubizarreta, who coauthored *Dancing Home*: https://www.youtube.com/watch?v=Tapnkf8WuGw. In this video, Alma Flor and Gabriel discuss their views of Latino culture, writing, and the power of language to help us all continue to develop deeper understandings of family and life together in this complicated world.

As I grow older and continue to dedicate my professional life to helping teachers gather the resources and develop the skills required to teach writing well, I am becoming increasingly passionate about providing children with access to books that show black and brown heroes. We must demand more books that feature historically marginalized people in brilliant-thinker roles and change-the-world roles. We give kids reason to dream by giving them access to great literature. I also know how critical it is for every child to connect personally with books and language. That means we must also demand more books that show everyday lives of people from all backgrounds. Every child needs not only to feel included but also to know the value of his or her cultural identity; every child needs to understand the importance of his or her peers' cultural background, too. Reading literature that highlights a variety of cultures broadens a person's worldview. Introducing books from many cultures is how we awaken the dreams of every young person.

Reading Like a Writer: The Use of Mentor Texts

The term *mentor* has a Greek origin from the *Odyssey*: Odysseus left his son, Telemachus, in the care of Mentor for his education and well-being. In today's world, we understand the term *mentor* to mean an experienced, wise, and trusted adviser or guide. Certainly this can be a person, but in the context of this text, it means authors of books and writings that, with the guidance of the teacher, can teach students how to write well. Books can be mentor texts only if we learn something about writing from them. And to make that learning accessible to students, we have to dig into the authors' works and note their moves. Then we try them out in our own writing—sometimes successfully and sometimes not, but always stretching and growing and learning about writing from these talented mentors. (Keep in mind, a mentor text can be any piece of writing—a website, a restaurant menu, a magazine article—but in this text we're focusing on children's books as mentor texts.)

Power resides in outstanding culturally diverse literature, too—power that has the potential to engage students in reading and teach them about the art and craft of writing. When students read high-quality and diverse books and materials, they have in their hands the very tools they need to improve their writing skills. It's a matter of reading like a writer.

Although the picture books and chapter books listed here can be used for teaching reading, I've gathered them as mentor texts for teaching writing. Pam Allyn (2015) writes, "Reading is like breathing in, writing is like breathing out" (1). I love this idea. My life's work has been teaching reading and writing simultaneously, focusing on craft as I go. No small feat, but oh so much easier, effective, and joyous than teaching reading and writing in isolation.

Gail E. Tompkins from *Literacy for the Twenty-First Century: A Balanced Approach* (2001) argues that there are three reasons reading and writing support each other: "1) readers and writers use the same intellectual strategies, 2) the reading and writing processes are similar, and 3) children use many of the same skills in both reading and writing" (31–32).

Frank Smith (1994), one of the first educational theorists to reveal the logic of using reading to teach writing, wrote, "There are three parties to every transaction that written language makes possible: a writer, a reader, and a text. And of the three, the text is the pivot . . . . Neither writers nor readers can exist without a text" (87). He further explains that "Reading like a writer is collaborative learning, even though it might appear that the reader is alone. But reading like a writer means reading with the author, as if one were writing the text oneself" (195–96).

The authors of the report *Writing Next*, Steve Graham and Dolores Perin (2007) also acknowledge the pivotal relationship between reading and writing. They present eleven essential elements to help students learn critical writing-literacy skills. Number ten on their list is "study of models," which urges teachers to provide students with opportunities to read, analyze, and emulate models of good writing. Their research not only supports the use of reading to improve writing but suggests a very specific way to accomplish it: using models. They say, "Students are encouraged to analyze these examples and to emulate the critical elements, patterns, and forms embodied in the models in their own writing" (20).

It simply makes sense to use the brilliant work of authors to teach writing and inspire students to write. Think of it as having an infinite number of extra hands helping you. Margarita Engle, Monica Brown, Duncan Tonatiuh, Pat Mora, F. Isabel Campoy, Pam Muñoz Ryan, Yuyi Morales, and a host of others are just waiting to be tapped for service. "Breathe in" and read the books by authors we admire. Then "breathe out" as you examine the authors' works for their writing craft.

Zeroing In on Children's Literature with Latino Themes as Mentor Texts for Writing

Chances are, if you've picked up this book (and you've read this far), you are or want to be a Dream Waker, and you realize how important diverse children's books are for our students. But chances are you've also encountered challenges in finding enough diverse children's books for your students. Me too. Over the last twenty years, I've created collections of picture books, chapter books, young adult literature, and "everyday texts" for teachers who understand the role reading plays in teaching writing. Considering what I've mentioned thus far, though, it has been a challenge to find high-quality material for young readers that feature Latino characters and culture. Yet almost every single time I conduct a workshop or make a presentation on using literature to teach writing, I'm asked if I can recommend a collection of books for Latino students, indeed for *all* students to celebrate Latino culture. The urgency feels particularly strong given the number of requests I've received recently and the number of times I've promised to make such a list.

In this spirit, I have compiled a list of mentor texts: picture books and chapter books that reflect Latino culture and feature Latino characters and themes. The books range from bilingual to English with Spanish words to English only. The majority were written by Latino authors, although some have been written by white authors who celebrate Latino culture. Some of these books you will love, and some you will not—for the same reasons that we don't all "ooh" and "ahh" over the same books in every other collection. I've read reviews, checked award lists, consulted Latino teachers, and read these books myself. In fact, I've been in hunter-gatherer mode for several years now. The books in this resource reflect a range of topics, reading levels, and interests. It's always important to remember, however, that you must read books yourself and decide for yourself whether they are appropriate to bring into your classroom. Ultimately, you are the professional educator who decides what works and what doesn't for your students.

I selected the books in *Dream Wakers* through a pretty rigorous and lengthy process, which you can read more about in Appendix A. As you will see, my personal experience is not the only sieve for deciding quality. I turned to experts in the field and read their opinions as I was forming my own. The process helped me gain confidence to select titles that represent high-quality literature reflective of Latino culture and life, something I would urge you to do as well because, in the end, you and your colleagues will be the ones making the critical decisions about which books to share with students. I'm simply the fortunate writer, reader, and educator who has collected and read all the books and wants to share them with you so that you can share them with all of your students, not just those who are Latino. The truth is, I still love *The Wizard of Oz* and *Charlotte's Web*, but I also treasure *The House on Mango Street*, *Maybe Something Beautiful*, and *Enchanted Airs*. Just wait—you will too.

EXPLORING LATINO LITERATURE WITH A WRITER'S EYE
By Alma Flor Ada

Words were the beginning. Words in the old ballads my mother sang at bedtime, in the poetry my grandmother shared, in my father's stories, in the gentle introduction to humankind's history.

Words took form when my grandmother traced them in the dirt to represent everything we saw on the farm, creating a story for each letter: *V* the *vaca* (cow) horn; *B* the *burro's* long ears; *R* the *rosa* escaping to see the world . . .

Words filled the pages in my first book, *Heidi*, an old, thick red volume my mother had kept. *Heidi* remained a favorite, read over and over. Nothing could have been farther from Cuba's tropical land than the snowed Alps. Yet, Heidi and I shared much. We both loved the nature surrounding us. Like Heidi, I spent long hours by myself, enthralled by observing everything around me. She delighted in the whispering of the wind in the pine trees, as I did listening to the wind whisper through the bamboo grove by the river. She looked forward to visiting the cabin of Peter's grandmother just as I enjoyed visiting my great-grandmother's humble house. The fact that both grandmothers were caring and blind made me feel a special kinship between us. Heidi could not accept living away from her mountains just as I could not imagine living far from the Quinta Simoni I loved so much.

My second-favorite book was *Mujercitas*, and I probably have been emulating Jo March for most of my life: as a free spirit ignoring conventionalism, as a caring daughter, as an aspiring writer, as a teacher of innovative ways.

But, much as I delighted in the stories of Louisa May Alcott and Frances Hodgson Burnett, the adventures of Salgari and Dumas, or the heartfelt experiences in De Amicis's *Corazón: Diario de un niño*, there was something I missed in my readings: the delightful rhythm of our Spanish language.

I later realized that all the stories I was reading were translations, and their language was stilted, devoid of the richness in the poetry of José Martí, of Rubén Darío, of Gabriela Mistral, or in the traditional tales as my grandmother told them.

Once I realized what the stories I read were missing, I began reinventing them in my mind, with my own words, hearing the sounds I was missing. And that led me to imagine further, to dream on the possibility of creating stories about the world around me . . .

Those childhood dreams led me later to enjoy translating as an art, the creation of versions in Spanish as engaging as the original, as well as to write stories of my own life and the lives of characters I know well.

No matter what I write, whether the protagonists are people, unicorns or hens, rabbits or birds, they will be authentic, because they have been born from real experiences, deeply felt.

I send my stories and poems out to the world wrapped in the hope that children will recognize some of their own feelings, questions, and fears, that my words may awaken their own dreams, offering validation and comfort, support and inspiration, just as books provided me in my childhood and have continued to do throughout life.

It's been an extraordinary journey, thanks to the encouragement of those great friends, intriguing and beguiling, rich in meaning and sound—wonderful words. ◉

The Traits of Writing and Mentor Texts

Learning to read like a writer is a matter of knowing what to look for. I use the traits of writing to help me explore texts for specific craft elements: ideas, organization, voice, word choice, sentence fluency, and conventions. The traits are the qualities that, when seamed together, make writing soar.

The traits give us a shared language to talk about writing, whether that writing was created by students or by children's authors.

The six traits of writing are the qualities that define good writing. They are present in every piece of writing regardless of the purpose. To write a strong informational or expository piece, for instance, a writer needs detailed ideas, an organizational plan, conviction and authority that creates voice, the right vocabulary, well-crafted sentences, and conventions of the language so the piece is readable to a broad audience. The traits allow us to get inside writing and see all the different moving pieces that make it work—or hold it back.

When we apply highly refined and clearly written scoring guides to student writing, we can clearly see the pathway to revision and editing. This is where the traits are most useful, providing consistent language and a guide that helps lead students to writing success through revision and editing. After all, if you can't pinpoint with accuracy and consistency what is working in the writing and what is not, how will students know what to do next to make it a stronger piece? Or, how will they know what techniques were successful so they can repeat them next time they write? I've written extensively about the power of using the traits as an assessment tool that leads to targeted instruction, and I urge you to read more in those resources if you are not familiar with them already.

 To download and try out the traits as an assessment tool and guide for teaching, you can visit www.culhamwriting.com. In the Library section on my website, you will find a tab for scoring guides customized for teachers as well as students. Please copy and share to your heart's content. You'll likely want these traits scoring guides on hand as you use the examples from this book as mentor texts.

If the traits are familiar, welcome them back into your thinking and teaching as you read and discuss *Dream Wakers*. If the traits are new to you, you've just gained a superpower to support writers at every age—because that's how the first encounter with the traits feels to writing teachers. As you read on, you'll discover definitions and explanations of the traits. Figure 1.2 provides a quick summary of each of the traits. You'll find more detailed definitions and examples at the start of each chapter as well.

As I've read and savored each of the books in this collection, I've come to appreciate how much celebrations are embedded in Latino culture. That made me wonder what it would look and feel like to hold a celebration for the traits, so I've added a little feature to this book that might make you smile and think metaphorically about them: a traits dinner party. I've come to know these traits so well, they are friends for life, so I invited them to

Figure 1.2 The Traits of Writing At a Glance

Ideas: The piece's content; its central message and details that support that message.

Organization: The internal structure of the piece—the thread of logic, the pattern of meaning.

Voice: The tone and tenor of the piece—the personal stamp of the writer, which is achieved through a strong understanding of purpose and audience.

Word Choice: The specific vocabulary the writer uses to convey meaning and enlighten the reader.

Sentence Fluency: The way words and phrases flow through the piece. It is the auditory trait and is therefore "read" with the ear as much as the eye.

Conventions: The mechanical correctness of the piece. Correct use of conventions (spelling, capitalization, punctuation, paragraphing, and grammar and usage) guides the reader through the text easily.

dinner and have written about each one's presence at our get-together. The hostess is Ideas, about whom you will read more in the next chapter. I think you'll like her, and you'll enjoy seeing how Ideas and her other trait friends intermingle when they get together.

Dream Wakers is organized by trait: ideas, organization, voice, word choice, sentence fluency, and conventions. In the world of writing, however, aligning books to a trait is not always as clean and straightforward as this organizational structure implies. After all, good writing is the combination of all the traits—all the different moves the author makes to create a clearly written piece. Good books, the ones I've chosen here, can be used as mentor texts for multiple traits. So to get you started, I've placed each book into a chapter based on my perception of its strongest trait; each annotation contains an idea for teaching that trait. However, each annotation also refers to a second trait that has a strong presence in the mentor text. You'll see these as abbreviations noted in parentheses at the end of each annotation (for example, I, O, V, WC, SF, and/or C). Please don't feel limited to my recommendations! As you become more comfortable with demonstrating traits of writing using mentor texts, you may find favorite books such as *Funny Bones: Posada and His Day of the Dead Calaveras* by Duncan Tonatiuh, or *Enchanted Air: Two Cultures, Two Wings* by Margarita Engle, that are worth dipping into again and again to show students many if not all of the traits in action.

The more you get to know a great book, the more you will see that is teachable to students. Keep in mind that there is no order or hierarchy for the traits. If you notice a particularly fluent phrase as you read, then it will work for sentence fluency. If you are struck by some element of the book's structure, then you'll have success using the book as a mentor for the organization trait. And sometimes, with the very best books, you'll see evidence of every trait and you'll come back to the book over and over, mining it for the precious ore between the covers. Few books have this distinction, but as a Dream Waker, you'll know them when you meet them.

Finding the Right Books at the Right Time

Here's a little organizational tip for your classroom library or personal children's book collection: Assign a color to each trait. As you find a book that is strong in that trait, put a small, colored sticker across the bottom of the spine of the book.

There are no official colors, of course, but below are the ones I use because it's easy to find stickers in these colors at local office supply stores:

Ideas—blue
Organization—orange
Voice—green
Word choice—red
Sentence fluency—turquoise
Conventions—purple

Most of my books are clearly labeled for one or more traits, because frankly, I live, breathe, and eat traits. In fact, some of my favorite books have six stickers on the spine! The majority, however, have only one or two.

So, how do you organize your books so you can make decisions as you prepare lessons? This is what works for me: Once a book is labeled, I write on the title page *why* I selected that book for that trait. A note might read, "Ideas: Great description on pages 17–88." Or, "Organization: Note the use of sequence words and transition words on pages 3–5." Or, "Voice: Shift in the tone of the voice on pages 7–10." Let's face it: the books you choose as mentor texts should have many, many strengths, so do yourself a favor and leave some clues about what craft in particular you can illustrate with each book. It will save you time later as you prepare your writing lessons and activities. Keep your stickers handy, too, because as you teach with a book over and over again, you'll likely find more specific uses for it with other traits.

Now that your books are stickered and labeled, you can file them in your classroom library for students to read and enjoy for any purpose they wish. But when the day comes that you are planning a focus lesson on a trait or a key quality of the trait, you won't have to search frantically for an example to show students. Just look at the stickers on the spines of the books, pull those that match the purpose of the lesson, and you'll be off and running. Cool, right?

Another organizational trick: buy file folders in the same colors as your stickers, and as you find cartoons, quotes, lessons, student paper examples, or anything else that might help teach students something about the trait, drop those resources into the color-coded folder. It works. Over the years, I've amassed quite a few files for each trait from which I draw ready-to-go resources for lessons.

A Word About Key Qualities

The traits are big concepts, so to make them easier to use and understand, I've broken each one down into four key qualities. These key qualities help us do two things: (1) assess the writing for one particular aspect of the trait and (2) zero in on a lesson or activity that will improve and support that key quality. In this way, we use the power of formative assessment to lead to focused instruction, and we do it in a manner that is focused, manage-able, and clear to teachers and students alike. After all, if we are looking for certain qualities in a student's writing to determine how he or she is pro-gressing, then we need to teach those same qualities to students with mean-ingful, practical ideas that improve their work. There should be no gray area between assessment and instruction: assess for the key qualities of these traits, then teach the key qualities. This is how students learn the art and craft of writing.

Key qualities allow us to be specific with students as they develop as writers. To comment about the organization of their text, for instance, is far too general to be helpful. What part of the organization of the text do you want them to think about: the beginning, the sequence and transitions, the structure of the body, the conclusion? It's critical that we home in and then offer an idea to move the piece forward. A nudge. A tip. A helpful, specific suggestion to try on their own. Ultimately, of course, we'll want the piece to show evidence of strength in all the traits and their key qualities, but we can accomplish this only by tackling the writing one key quality at a time: catch and release. Build understanding over time to create confident, skilled writers.

One of the best methods for teaching students about each trait's key qualities is through mentor texts. We examine the mentor text for evidence of the trait and one or more of the key qualities, identify passages where we help students see it done by a master, analyze and have conversations about it, and then help students try the writer's moves out for themselves. The key qualities are what make aspects of the trait more touchable and understandable for students and teachers alike. Without them, each trait is a vast ocean—perhaps a specific ocean such as the Pacific, but still so big and broad it is overwhelming. Key qualities allow us to break the trait into more manageable writing components much like the points on a writing compass that guides you along the way. At the start of each chapter that follows, I describe key qualities of the featured trait and provide some guidance on what to look for when choosing mentor texts on your own.

Getting Started with *Dream Wakers*

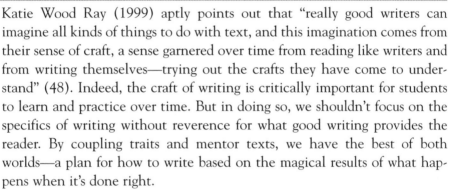

Katie Wood Ray (1999) aptly points out that "really good writers can imagine all kinds of things to do with text, and this imagination comes from their sense of craft, a sense garnered over time from reading like writers and from writing themselves—trying out the crafts they have come to understand" (48). Indeed, the craft of writing is critically important for students to learn and practice over time. But in doing so, we shouldn't focus on the specifics of writing without reverence for what good writing provides the reader. By coupling traits and mentor texts, we have the best of both worlds—a plan for how to write based on the magical results of what happens when it's done right.

On a practical level, there is no foolproof recipe or all-purpose technique for matching a mentor text to a writing trait. You must know the facets of the trait and its key qualities and read a potential mentor text with the same focus that a jeweler uses with a loupe. Try to spot connections. I have many picture books that I love but don't use for teaching writing because nothing clicks as I look at them for specific lesson planning. That's fine. Books are glorious for many different reasons. But as you read a book, ask yourself if the author has created a piece that is teachable for writing, not just for reading. To answer that question, you must read with a writer's eye, looking for clues for how the book was written, what techniques are clearly visible to the reader, and how you can help students become better writers by bringing the author's craft into their writing lives.

The following chapters focus on what each trait is all about, how to select mentor texts for teaching writing, and where you'll find books that celebrate Latino culture to use to teach the trait and its key qualities. You'll also glean insights into the authors who wrote them. The entire recommended book list consists of 120 picture books and chapter books that will appeal to children in upper-elementary grades. Each picture book and chapter book annotation contains

- bibliographic information;
- a brief summary of what makes the book special;
- a notation of traits that are strongest; and
- an idea you can use to teach the craft of writing.

Because chapter books are so much longer than picture books, I created a separate list for them and include an excerpt that shows strength in particular traits. I also provide a teaching idea to use with the passage to get you started.

Chapters are organized by trait, too, so you can dip in and out throughout your instruction—consider these "just in time" resources to use with students; as you notice areas where students need support, these books and lessons are standing by. And there is an at-a-glance chart in Appendix B that provides key information for quick reference. Ideally, you can use it to quickly locate books and information about them.

Throughout the book, there are original, delicious, and insightful writings by respected authors who write about Latino lives, stories, culture, and themes. They discuss their writing process, what motivates them to write, the importance of diverse texts for all students, the themes that matter most to them, where their inspiration is found, and oh so much more! These essays alone are worthy of study, and I encourage you to read them aloud to your students and share them with colleagues. They are fresh and filled with the passion and voice of the authors' published works, only these are specially written to you. No matter where you live and work and irrespective of the cultural background of your students, you'll glean special insight into the beauty and meaning of the authors' books from their personal essays about their motivations to write.

It's hard for me to say what I love best about this book. As I've been deeply engaged in finding and reading books that feature Latino culture, I've fallen in love over and over and over with different titles—and it's been exhilarating to think about ideas for teaching to go with them. The author essays have moved me tremendously. Each author's passion for writing about Latino lives, locales, and traditions is undeniable. When you read their books and then their words about writing, trust me, you'll get goose bumps.

I hope *Dream Wakers* will inspire you and your students in your critical work together. You give them permission to dream through stories and information that inspires and teaches, awakening the desire for rich and fulfilling lives of their own. This is the power of books. In this text, it is my dream for you, the reader, to understand and appreciate the beauty of Latino culture—for all students, Latino or not. You'll undoubtedly fall in love with some of these books, just as I did. I only wish I were there by your side as you open the covers and fall in. Celebrate the worlds and words of the Dream Wakers who provide us this beautiful collection of books to share with students everywhere. I invite you to immerse yourself in books that celebrate a culture of beauty and warmth, tradition and love, family and joy.

Let's begin.

RANDOM SHOTS THAT HIT THE MARK
By Joe Hayes

When I attempt to explain to myself, or to others, why so many of the stories I tell are derived from the Hispanic oral tradition, an old tale comes to mind. It's a story about a renowned marksman. The tale turns up in many cultures around the world:

A famous rifleman arrives one day at a certain village, and on a wall at the edge of town he sees evidence that someone has used it for target practice. The unknown shooter appears to have drawn small bull's-eyes, not much bigger around than a bullet, on the wall and shot at them. Remarkably, his bullet has hit right in the center of each bull's-eye! The great marksman is impressed. Not even he could shoot that well. He inquires in the village for the shooter's identity.

"It's the boy Juanito," he's told. "He's always taking target practice with his father's rifle."

The famous rifleman soon locates the boy and asks for a demonstration of his remarkable skill. They return to the wall, and the boy stations himself at a distance of about fifty paces. He blasts away with his father's rifle. Then he walks up to the wall, takes a piece of chalk from his pocket, and draws a circle around the crater made by each bullet he has fired.

My thoughts about the value of sharing Hispanic stories are like those bull's-eyes drawn after the shots were already fired. I began as a storyteller like the boy Juanito, just tossing out the stories I liked to whatever listeners happened to be in front of me. Often they were Hispanic children in schools in New Mexico. By observing the children's reactions, I was able to draw a circle of accuracy around certain stories. The children showed me which stories really hit the mark.

If the story I told was a Hispanic story, a *cuento*—one I had developed from memories of growing up in a small town in Arizona, or one I'd constructed from material collected by folklorists who documented the traditional tales of New Mexico in the early 1900s—I could see a special glow of appreciation come over the faces of the Latino children. When I seasoned the telling with phrases in Spanish, their physical appearance quite literally changed. They sat up higher, looking around them with pride at their ability to understand every word. I knew I was right on target.

I also observed that non–Spanish-speakers seemed to show an uncharacteristic interest in the story and the language—hence in the culture. We were all feeling a sense of community. That's why I have continued to concentrate on such stories ever since—not because there's a market for Hispanic-oriented stories, and not because I have any sense of ownership of the tradition, but because I enjoy the stories and see that they do good work.

In the beginning I carried all the stories in my head and shared them only orally, but soon listeners, especially teachers, began encouraging me to write the stories. I began to realize that I could share the stories more widely by publishing them. I love telling that to children, and I often make them repeat after me: *Writing is sharing.* I tell them that if they write about what interests them, they can share it with people who live far away, even in places they'll never visit. I especially enjoy telling about an e-mail I received from a librarian in Buenos Aires, Argentina. She wanted me to know that she had read one of my books to a student who had no interest in learning to read. But somehow the story touched the right spot in him. "*Quiero aprender a leer esta historia,*" he told her: "I want to learn to read this story." *Writing is sharing,* I emphasize to the children, and you never know when something you have written will make a difference in another person's life.

To write my first book, *The Day It Snowed Tortillas,* I sat at a typewriter (yes, it was that long ago) and listened to myself tell the stories in my imagination as I wrote them. My hope was that readers would hear a voice telling the stories in their minds as they read them. And that led to the second idea I emphasize with children: *Write with your ears.* The biggest mistake you can make when you write is to not listen to yourself. The language you use when you talk and the language you use when you write are the same language. The beauty of writing is that you can revise it. When you talk, you often don't say things the way you wish you had. Later, you think, *I should have said that differently.* When you write, you get to say things in your I-wish-I-had-said way.

Finally, I stress that you enjoy talking about things you like, things that interest and satisfy you. Write about them. I've always been drawn to the traditional tales of the Hispanic Southwest, and so I tell and write them. My motivation isn't political, or economic. I share stories that give me joy, and feel very fortunate that they sometimes give joy to others—especially that they're well received and appreciated by Hispanic children. ✪

Chapter 2

THE CENTER OF ATTENTION

IDEAS

For years, teachers have asked me where to start when they work with the traits. And for years, I've told them that it really doesn't matter—you can jump in with any trait and make terrific writing gains right away. But truthfully, over time I've come to realize that until the writer has an idea, the other traits need to huddle around the developing idea, supporting and waiting their turn to be in the spotlight. In other words, Ideas would be the hostess at the traits dinner party; she dedicates herself to making sure that, ultimately, it's a successful evening for all.

The ideas trait is all about the content—the central message and the details that support that message. Writing shows strength in ideas when its topic is clear and narrow, and its details are specific, interesting, and accurate. Because the writer knows what he or she wants to say and anticipates the reader's questions, the piece is focused, well developed, and full of original thinking.

To accomplish this, writers must develop skills in each of the following key qualities of the ideas trait:

- **Finding a Topic:** The writer offers a clear, central theme or simple, original story line that is memorable.

- **Focusing the Topic:** The writer narrows the theme or story line to create a piece that is clear, tight, and manageable.
- **Developing the Topic:** The writer provides enough critical evidence to support the theme and show insight into the topic. Or he or she tells the story in a fresh way through an original, unpredictable plot.
- **Using Details:** The writer offers credible, accurate details that create pictures in the reader's mind. Those details provide the reader with evidence of the writer's knowledge about and/or experience with the topic.

You may remember a reference in Chapter 1 to a light hearted feature in each trait chapter called the traits dinner party. I've added it to give you a fresh look at each trait and its relationship to others—a metaphor for how the traits come together in a piece of writing. The traditional definitions of the traits are clear and helpful, no doubt. But at the dinner party, I've personified each trait to bring them to life as characters who know one another and socialize. Between the customary understanding of the traits and the dinner party, you'll get to know each trait individually and as a group—and maybe find a new favorite.

The Traits Dinner Party: Ideas

Welcome to the traits dinner party! Our host, Ideas, clearly enjoys the arrival of the guests and greets each trait warmly. She did, after all, invite only compatible colleagues to the dinner party and wants everyone to enjoy their time together. Wearing a long shimmering dress, her hair swept back neatly but not fussily, she looks every bit the person in charge. She wears dangly earrings and opera beads. As Ideas settles into her place at the head of the table, presiding over the meal, it's clear she is taller than the other guests and is a dominating presence in the room. And she throws her head back when she laughs—just another way to command attention.

As the meal gets under way, you'll notice how Ideas cleverly responds to everyone's questions in an ongoing stream of conversation punctuated by stories and information that delight and enlighten everyone around her. She is well informed and able to converse on a variety of topics with expertise and credibility. The range of what she knows, actually, is quite impressive. Word Choice chimes in to add details and descriptions, while

Voice listens intently, adding insightful comments and anecdotes that help personalize the topic to each trait's point of view. The flow of the ideas is natural and easy to follow, thanks to Organization's ability to help guests stay on track as he makes connections from one trait's thinking to another. Sentence Fluency speaks eloquently about subjects and smacks her hand on the table, adding "Yes!" when in agreement with others. Conventions points out when one trait or another is dominating the conversation too much, reminding the guests that there are rules for polite conversation that should be followed. He's a bit of a downer, but he's a good moderator.

Mostly, however, this evening shows Ideas at her best. She brings up timely topics and asks for the guests to speak to specific issues about them as the discussions become rich with new, insightful information. Her stories and anecdotes entertain and engage the listeners. She's a charming hostess and much adored by all.

Choosing Mentor Texts for the Ideas Trait

A picture book is ideal for writing-craft study. Picture books are relatively short and model how to do a lot with a little. Chapter books, on the other hand, can feel daunting. To use a chapter book as a mentor text, pick a passage or a paragraph for further examination, not a chapter—and certainly not the whole book. Ideally, no matter your choice—shorter or longer—students will enjoy reading it with you, and as they discover the secrets on its pages, they'll ask to borrow the book and read it on their own. This is the winning Powerball ticket of reading and writing instruction: students *choosing* to read more and, therefore, learn more.

Finding the books that will work best for you and your students takes practice and imagination. You have to see the possibilities. When prowling the pages of a picture book or chapter book for the ideas trait, think about the creativity and workmanship that lie between the covers and how the author conveys the major ideas of the piece. Look for words and phrases and pages that can help you teach students how to write in ways that answer the following questions about key qualities for the ideas trait:

Finding a Topic: What is the book about? What's the big idea? Why did the author choose this topic—are there clues about a personal connection or other reason? Does it make you wonder about related topics or stories that might develop from the big idea in the text?

Focusing the Topic: Think about where the idea might have originated. How did the author go from a big, general idea, such as animals, to one particular magical fish and its story? Or to a comparison and contrast piece about animals with special capabilities and which is the most powerful? What other options might this author have considered for this book's focus?

Developing the Topic: How much information or story development did the author provide to make the idea clear? Were your questions answered? Did the author share his or her fascination with the idea in an interesting and accurate way? Did you find yourself drawn into the idea in a particular place?

Using Details: Which details take the book's idea out of the realm of the ordinary and into the extraordinary? What original details make the writing memorable and help you think about the topic in a fresh, new way? Are they sensory? When you close your eyes and think about the ideas in the book, which details still dance in your mind?

Strong Ideas Are More Than Prompts

As you read and consider the following books for the different key qualities of the ideas trait, don't feel boxed in by the topic. The books are here to be considered as mentor texts, not as copycat books. Students shouldn't attempt to write about the same topic as the mentor text; that's the author's idea, and it's already been handled masterfully. However, the mentor text can inspire new ideas. Work with students and use your imagination and creativity to think about what is possible using the mentor text as a springboard for writing—not as a prompt. There is a difference. Students will never give us their best thinking when we tell them what to write. Instead, inspire them with possibilities that stem from the mentor texts.

Adhering to a prompt and teaching the ideas trait get muddled in our assessments and the comments we give to students. Prompts tend to have a perceived endgame in mind. Teachers have said to me, "The topic in this piece is pretty good, but it doesn't follow the prompt. So that's a low score in ideas, right?" These teachers are responding to how well the student followed the directions, not the ideas trait. Instead, leave room for a paper that is strong in ideas but perhaps takes a turn that is different from what is expected. This is actually a good thing: the prompt is doing its real job, which is to assist or encourage the writer to say something of significance.

I'm no fan of directed writing prompts, because they fail to provide the writer any mental elbow room. In fact, I rather abhor them. I call these *closed-end prompts* because they shut off thinking; the task becomes trying to write something that the reader/evaluator is looking for—not what the writer really has to say. And the minute we do that, writing is no longer authentic. I know that closed-end prompts are a part of our assessment world, so to that I say, teach students how to write well using best practices, including the use of mentor texts. Then right before the high-stakes test, show them the format and the rules they must follow, and let them get comfortable with them. Approach the test prompt like a genre of writing. But don't be fooled into thinking this is good writing practice. It's not. As soon as the test is over, get back to brilliant teaching.

I believe that this prompt issue has been the de facto assessment tool in writing classes and on standardized tests for years and years: High grades go to students who nailed the prompt and what the evaluators expected to see, and lower grades go to those who didn't. In other words, we don't really assess the writing; we assess how closely the student came to giving us the answer we asked for in writing.

Give students feedback on the quality of their writing first. Tell them if the idea they wrote about is clear, focused, developed, and uses details—regardless of the topic they write about. Radical, right? Then tell them if they've strayed from the directions and why that matters (if it does). Separate these two issues—following the directions and their ability to handle an idea—and you'll find it a lot simpler to communicate to students what is working in their writing itself and what still needs work.

If we loosen the reins of what we encourage students to do with their ideas, if we help them dig into a topic and find out what fascinates them about it, and if we give them permission to pursue their interests, then we'll have better writers with lifelong skills that transfer to whatever topics they write about in the future. And, as a bonus, we'll have fewer cookie-cutter writing pieces, covering the same information in the same way—boring. (Just imagine how much more fun you'll have when faced with reading a pile of student writing, as well!) I am going out on a limb here, but I don't think tightly prompted writing is worthy of students' and teachers' time and energy. Prompted writing is all about "guessing it right" to get a good grade; it's not thinking and questioning and growing as a writer with freedom to fail as part of accepted practice.

As you explore the books in this chapter, I challenge you to discover those that you find stunningly written and inspiring, as I found Duncan Tonatiuh's *Funny Bones: Posada and His Day of the Dead Calveras* the first time I read it . . . then the second and the third. Consider the possibilities of where this book might take your student writers if you abandoned the dreaded *P* word and focused on strong ideas and how to write them clearly. Might some students get excited about creating a different historical account of how something came to be? Or uncovering a process that requires step-by-step directions? Exploring questions to be answered in an opinion piece on related but different topics? These three modes exist in Tonatiuh's story: narrative, informative, and opinion. All three are modeled brilliantly. Use mentor texts to spark kids' imaginations about what they might write about and fan the flames of possibility. Choice is critical to writing success.

WHERE IDEAS COME FROM: THE STORY OF BIBLIOBURRO
By Jeanette Winter

I read the newspaper every morning.

I read the paper to get the news from all around the world and the news from my small part of the world.

Sometimes I get ideas when I read the newspaper—ideas for my books, and ideas for the pictures that will tell the story in my books.

The story of *Biblioburro* came from the newspaper. The morning I read about Luis and his traveling library, I immediately knew I wanted to write a book about Luis and his books. And I wanted to make pictures of Colombia—the mountains, the flowers, the children waiting for books from the biblioburro, Luis and Diana, the two burros.

The first thing I do is gather all the material I can find to help me tell the story. I looked on the Internet to see if there were any more news stories about Luis. I searched for pictures of Colombia and the small town of La Gloria, where Luis lives, and pictures of the plants that grow there. When I'm working on a book, I listen to music from the place that I'm writing about, so I looked for CDs of Colombian music. The music helps me feel like I'm there, where the story is happening.

When I've thought about the story and pictures for a while (sometimes for a long time, sometimes just for a day or two), I begin.

Some of my books start with me making the pictures, but with *Biblioburro*, I started with the words. When I had a rough draft of the whole story, I made very small, very rough sketches of the pictures I would paint.

Next I started working on the paintings, finishing each one before going on to the next.

And then, I went back to the story, and changed words, and added words, and subtracted words, until I felt it was just right.

And I looked again at the pictures and sometimes changed a few details, or even made a new picture, until I felt they were just right.

In a picture book, going back and forth between the text and the pictures is an important part of telling the story.

The pictures can tell things that the words don't, and the words tell what the pictures can't.

And now . . . I'm going to read my newspaper.

I never know what I'm going to find there! ◉

Mentor Texts for the Ideas Trait: Picture Books

Books are listed alphabetically in every trait chapter and are listed comprehensively on an at-a-glance chart in Appendix B. Along with other key information about each book, I've selected a dominant trait and a secondary trait and tried to zero in on the key quality for teaching. But remember, don't let my choices override your own. If you see teaching possibilities for other traits in any of these marvelous books, make note of those areas as well. The key for my picks is simple:

I—Ideas
O—Organization
V—Voice
WC—Word Choice
SF—Sentence Fluency
C—Conventions

The Barking Mouse
Written by Antonio Sacre
Illustrated by Alfredo Aguirre
Albert Whitman, 2003

On the surface, here's a simple tale of Mamá, Papá, Sister, and Brother Ratón, a mouse family, who go on a picnic and find delightful ways to entertain themselves. The message of the book, however, is what attracted me to it—not just the story. Mamá says, "You see, kids? ¡Es muy importante hablar otro idioma! It pays to speak another language!" The author's note before the story is worth reading and discussing. Many students will relate to Antonio Sacre's thinking and his personal experiences learning two languages that inspired *The Barking Mouse*.

Explore the author's note with students, paying attention to how the story idea shows up in different versions from Cuba and Uruguay. Sacre notes that another version features an American mouse and an American cat. Ask them to write about whether they agree or disagree that "language is the key to surviving the difficulties of a new place." (I, WC)

Black and Blanco! Engaging Art in English y Español
artekids.org
Trinity University Press, 2013

I was surprised to discover several board books with high-level thinking and vocabulary. Traditionally, this genre has been reserved for simple texts that are an introduction to more complex concepts. Not so here. The striking artwork is intertwined with thoughts and inspiring questions that will allow readers to imagine and explore their own questions on related ideas. As new words are introduced in English and Spanish, readers are drawn into the meaning by a question that explores further thinking about the word's meaning.

Read the book and let students see how it is organized: the English word, the Spanish word, a question to explore the meaning of the word. Have students select another word in English and Spanish and write a question that gives the reader a focus for deeper understanding of the meaning. (I, WC)

Dalia's Wondrous Hair/El cabello maravilloso de Dalia
Written and Illustrated by Laura Lacámara
Spanish translation by Gabriela Baenza Ventura
Piñata Books, 2014

Dalia is determined to use her beautiful, long locks for something that will surprise everyone—even her mama. She holds everyone in suspense until one day, the secret is exposed and family and friends have to agree: Dalia, indeed, has wondrous hair! This bilingual text is bound to delight readers as they imagine the possibilities for writing based on *Dalia's Wondrous Hair*.

The secret of Dalia's hair is a surprise for the reader. Ask students to think of something else that could be hidden in Dalia's hair and write about how it would be revealed in a sequel to this amusing story. (I, WC)

Doña Flor: A Tall Tale About a Giant Woman with a Great Big Heart/ Doña Flor: un cuento de una mujer gigante con un gran corazón

Written by Pat Mora
Illustrated by Raul Colón
Dragonfly Books, 2005
Pura Belpré Award, Pura Belpré Honor Book,
Golden Kite Award

There was never a woman more giving and kind than Doña Flor. Readers discover her enormous capacity to give to humans, animals, and the natural world—and her enormous size. She is a giant, after all. This tall tale is bound to delight, amuse, and inspire readers of every age.

Ask students to compare Doña Flor with another tall-tale character they may know: Paul Bunyan. Have them make a chart comparing Doña Flor's qualities with Paul Bunyan's. Then, have students write a short piece expressing their opinions about which giant they would rather meet and why. (I, V)

¡El Cucuy! A Bogeyman Cuento in English and Spanish

As Told by Joe Hayes
Illustrated by Honorio Robledo
Cinco Puntos, 2002
Independent Publisher Ippy Award

Growing up, everyone heard about the "bogeyman." In this folktale he's known as el Cucuy. El Cucuy's job was to be the horrible scary creature your parents threatened you with if you were lazy or disobedient. In this bilingual tale, readers find out what happened to bad little boys and girls when el Cucuy had to come down from the mountains to carry them off.

Have students draw a picture of what el Cucuy looks like from the description in the story. Then, have them explain to a younger brother, sister, or family friend why they should look out for el Cucuy and what to do to avoid ever having to see him. (I, V)

Floating on Mama's Song/Flotando en la canción de mamá

Written by Laura Lacámera
Illustrated by Yuyi Morales
Katherine Tegen Books, 2010

Magical themes are part of this lyrical bilingual text. As a narrative, it presents a clear problem: Anita's mama loves to sing, but it seems as though her singing is causing some odd things to happen. So she stops. Anita's mission is to find a way to bring singing back into their lives to restore the great happiness it brings.

Students will love the magic in this text. Ask them to think of another gift someone might have, such as extraordinary sports skills, painting or sculpting skills, or writing skills, and then to create a character with that gift and a problem and solution that results from it. Ask them to focus on the solution so they see how their idea and the organization of the idea work together. (I, O)

Hairs and Pelitos
Written by Sandra Cisneros
Illustrated by Terry Ybáñez
Translated from English by Liliana Valenzuela
Dragonfly Books, 1984

One chapter from *The House on Mango Street* has been turned into a sensory-filled bilingual picture book. Touching moments that recall a family's distinctly different hair make this text a beautiful piece to share and celebrate the similarities and differences between people—family or not.

Taking one small idea—hair—and turning it into a picture book means using many specific details to develop the topic. Explore the range of senses (taste, touch, see, feel, hear) used to communicate the idea in the text. Ask students to write about their name and where it comes from using the same level of focus, detail, and expressiveness. (I, WC)

If the Shoe Fits
Written by Gary Soto
Illustrated by Terry Widener
Putnam Juvenile, 2002

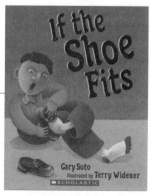

Rigo's mother surprises him with new shoes—his first pair ever—but other kids ridicule and tease him about how they look. So he puts his fancy new shoes in the closet, and by the time he pulls them out again for a special party, they are way too small.

Ask students to discuss how important it is to them to have just the right clothes or shoes and how it makes them feel if they are teased or bullied about what they wear. Encourage them to write an opinion piece to persuade bullies to leave them alone, keep their opinions to themselves, and be more positive in their interactions. (I, V)

In My Family: En mi familia
Written and Illustrated by Carmen Lomas Garza
Spanish translation by Francisco X. Alarcón
Children's Book Press, 1996
Pura Belpré Honor Book, Tomás Rivera Mexican Children's Book Award

Author and artist Carmen Lomas Garza begins the book with an author's note in which she explains, "When I was growing up . . . [w]e were punished for being who we were, and we were made to feel ashamed of our culture." This book of family pictures and memories honors Garza's culture and gives readers a glimpse into her rich and loving family life growing up near the US/Mexico border.

Have students pick a favorite picture and read more about it on trustworthy Internet sites and by using other credible resources. Ask them to find at least three more interesting details and facts, write the additional information about their selection, and share it with the class. Some of the topics that might intrigue them from the book are horned toads, *nopalitos*, *empanadas*, piñatas, *cascarones*, *ventosa*, *curandera*, the La Llorona legend, and the story of the Virgin of Guadalupe. (I, WC)

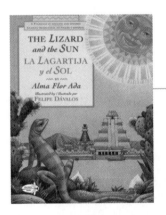

The Lizard and the Sun/La lagartija y el sol
Written by Alma Flor Ada
Illustrated by Felipe Dávalos
Dragonfly Books, 2007

The legend tells the tale of the brave lizard who found the sun sleeping. He was responsible for waking the sun and making it shine with warmth and life for all living plants and creatures. In this bilingual text, readers explore the importance of the sun for all living things.

Have students write about the prospect of water or fire disappearing for good. Ask them to write a legend about how water or fire could be saved by one person or animal using the legend structure modeled in *The Lizard and the Sun*. (I, O)

A Mango in the Hand: A Story Told Through Proverbs
Written by Antonio Sacre
Illustrated by Sebastia Serra
Abrams, 2011

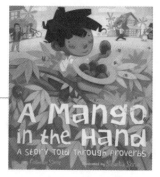

Proverbs—"short pithy saying[s] in general use, stating a general truth or piece of advice" (Google Dictionary Online)—are scattered throughout as Francisco's misadventures gathering mangos for his saint day celebration take him through an unexpected series of events. Told in English with many Spanish words and phrases throughout, the story is bound to delight readers of all ages. It can give the class opportunities to explore proverbs and what they mean so that when students encounter proverbs in other reading, they will understand how they work.

Ask students to work in pairs and select one of the proverbs from the story. Have them reread the context of the proverb in *A Mango in the Hand* and discuss what the proverb intends for the reader to understand about life at that moment in the book. Then have them explore what the proverb means as truth or advice in the bigger world of life and language. Invite students to create a short scenario where their proverb would apply and share their stories with other classmates. (I, WC)

Marisol McDonald Doesn't Match/Marisol McDonald no combina
Written by Monica Brown
Illustrated by Sara Palacios
Lee and Low Books, 2011
Pura Belpré Honor Book

Marisol is the most unmatched girl in the universe, and she likes it that way. However, she decides to try to match and see how life would change. She finds, in this splendid bilingual text, that it is best to be who we are and embrace our differences and celebrate them.

Use the theme of this book to play a game. Point out four different areas of the room and ask a question with four different choices. Students move to the corner with the answer that best matches their response. For example, "Which snack do you prefer?" Corner 1, chips; Corner 2, candy; Corner 3, vegetables; Corner 4, fruit. Ask at least five different questions and then have students write about what they discovered about the likes and dislikes of classmates and how they matched up with their own. (I, O)

Maybe Something Beautiful: How Art Transformed a Neighborhood
Written by F. Isabel Campoy and Theresa Howell
Illustrated by Rafael López
Houghton Mifflin Harcourt, 2016

There are books that grab your heart and don't let go. This is one for me. The message is one of joy and hope, the words and phrases sing off the page, and the illustrations are simply stunning. Based on a true story from the East Village in San Diego, California, this book tells how one neighborhood found its voice through art. Don't miss the end notes that explain the Urban Art Trail and its movement. "Maybe . . . just maybe" readers of this book will be inspired to see the possibilities of life and community through art and volunteer in their own communities to replicate this project.

Color and movement drive the illustrations and the ideas for this book. Ask students to pick favorite pages and write about the significance of each to them, the readers. They should describe how they feel when they read. Invite them to write with passion, using words and color to make their ideas stand out. (I, V)

My Diary from Here to There/Mi diaro de aqui hasta allá
Written by Amada Irma Pérez
Illustrated by Maya Christina Gonzalez
Lee and Low Books, 2002
Pura Belpré Honor Book

The thought of moving to the United States, leaving behind everything she knows and *everyone* she knows—including her best friend—is daunting to a young girl. Our young protagonist writes about the events of her move as well as her thoughts and feelings in this fictional diary-formatted book. Expressing realistic fears and concerns, this story is gentle and honest.

Journals can be a helpful way for students to express what matters to them about their everyday lives. Plan two weeks (including weekends) for students to keep a daily journal of all the interesting things they do and with whom. Have them use as many details as possible to paint a picture of what these experiences are like. After two weeks, have them write a summary of what the journal reveals about what they enjoy doing the most and note if the journal helped to uncover any surprises. (I, O)

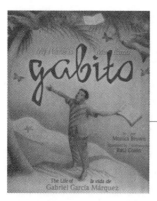

My Name Is Gabito/Me llamo Gabito: The Life of Gabriel García Márquez
Written by Monica Brown
Illustrated by Raúl Colón
Luna Rising, 2007
Pura Belpré Honor Book

Gabito was a writer who could paint pictures in a reader's mind using the most magnificent words and phrases. He could bring any idea to life. In this bilingual biography, readers get a taste of Gabriel García Márquez's creativity and imagination. It's more than a taste—it's a feast for the eyes and the mind.

In the first part of the book, Brown offers expanded paragraphs about individual events that were important to Gabito. Each is followed by a one-line summary. Ask students to take the questions on page 1 and the questions on the last six pages of the book and write colorful, descriptive passages followed by a one-line summary similar to those modeled in the body of the text. (I, O, WC)

My Very Own Room/Mi propio cuartito
Written by Amada Irma Pérez
Illustrated by Maya Christina Gonzalez
Lee and Low Books, 2000
Tomás Rivera Mexican American Children's Book Award

Living in a family of eight can be a challenge on its own—but having to share a bedroom with five brothers leaves the nine-year-old daughter yearning for a room of her own. In this gentle and loving bilingual story based on the author's life, tiny but perfect space is found, painted, and furnished so a young girl can have the much-needed privacy her family knows she deserves.

Ask students to think of a place in their own house that is small, unseen, and treasured like the one in My Very Own Room. If they don't have such a spot, can they imagine one? Or choose a treasured spot from their yard or a vacation place or a friend's house? Then ask students to write an opinion piece about why that space should be their new room: what would they do to change it into a magical place where they could go to dream, read, and write? (I, V)

Napí
Written by Antonio Ramírez
Illustrated by Domi
Douglas and McIntyre, 2004

Domi is one of my favorite illustrators. His art brings simple stories to life with rich and imaginative details artfully placed on every page—and the color palette is simply scrumptious, a perfect choice for this English picture book with Spanish words. The book also has a Spanish version. The simple story line uses color to highlight ideas from Napí's imagination as she listens to her grandfather's stories and then dreams on—becoming the heron who flies freely along the riverbank, taking in the natural world.

Discuss with students how the art and the ideas in this text are intertwined. Ask them to select several spreads and look at them closely; use a document camera, if possible, so the whole class can examine together. Make a list of details that support the main idea of the page and focus on the use of color. Have students then go to a piece of their own writing and add details that elaborate on the big idea. Have them illustrate the text by drawing, adding collage, painting with watercolors, or some other method they prefer, highlighting those details. (I, WC)

Pablo Neruda: Poet of the People
Written by Monica Brown
Illustrated by Julie Paschkis
Henry Holt, 2011

Pablo was a poet of his people: from his youth, the written word was his best friend. He stood up for what was right and pledged his loyalty to helping his Chilean countrymen. This biography draws readers into Pablo Neruda's passion for life and language as revealed in his remarkable poetry.

Ask students to help you find examples of Pablo Neruda's poems in books from the library or on Internet sites. Read several that are the most appealing to the class, and discuss them. Then ask students to write a blog post about what makes Neruda's poems so powerful. (I, V, WC)

Pancho Rabbit and the Coyote: A Migrant's Tale
Written and Illustrated by Duncan Tonatiuh
Abrams, 2013

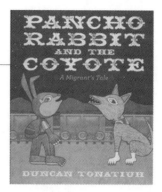

It's not money or gifts Pancho wants; it's the safe return of his father, who has traveled north to find work and send money home. A great adventure ensues when Pancho encounters the trickster coyote after he sets out to find his father.

The trickster coyote is a familiar character in Latino tales—he's wily and always stirs up trouble. Ask students to create a "wanted" poster of the trickster coyote and identify as many details as possible about him so others can identify him and turn him in! (I, WC)

Parrots Over Puerto Rico
Written by Susan L. Roth and Cindy Trumbore
Illustrated by Susan L. Roth
Lee and Low Books, 2013
The Robert F. Siebert Medal, America's Award for Children's and Young Adult Literature

Richly illustrated and written in a lively style, this book is jam-packed with information about Puerto Rican parrots, including the history of these birds, their struggle for survival, and a brief history of the island of Puerto Rico itself. *Parrots Over Puerto Rico* describes the extensive recovery efforts to bring the species back from the brink of extinction—and the happy result. The afterword provides information about the Puerto Rican parrot species and the recovery program dedicated to protecting them. It shouldn't be missed.

Students will be fascinated by the success of the Puerto Rican Parrot Recovery Program and may be aware that other endangered species need the same support. Encourage kids to read further about efforts to save another animal from extinction and to write to animal welfare organizations in support of what they are doing or to ask how to help. (I, V)

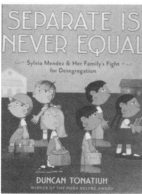

Separate Is Never Equal: Sylvia Mendez and Her Family's Fight for Desegregation
Written and illustrated by Duncan Tonatiuh
Abrams, 2014
Pura Belpré Award

Students today may not fully realize that schools in the United States were once segregated. This historical and biographical book documents the importance of a 1947 California ruling that paved the way for national desegregation laws. It illustrates in beautiful prose and pictures the struggles of the Mendez family, highlighting specifically the work of Sylvia Mendez, who sought justice and choice for all children. A detailed author's note at the end will give students the historical context they will need to understand the significance of Sylvia Mendez's voice in a little-known event in American history.

Ask students if they agree with the title, *Separate Is Never Equal*, and have them write with a partner a short statement about their position. Remind students to clearly state their opinion and provide evidence from the text to support their position for why they feel the way they do. Students should have a round-table discussion that allows all members to express their ideas and back them up using examples and information. (I, V)

A Spoon for Every Bite/Una cuchara para cada bocado
Written by Joe Hayes
Illustrated by Rebecca Leer
Cinco Puntos, 2005
Land of Enchantment Book Award

Readers explore poverty and wealth in this bilingual story. The husband and wife protagonists are poor, so poor they only have two spoons. They have a rich neighbor who boasts that he has enough money to buy so many spoons, he never has to use the same one twice. He runs out of money proving his wealth, however, and in the end, the young couple wind up with all of his spoons to sell and they become rich themselves.

Ask students to figure out the moral of the story. Then ask them to decide if it is ethical for the husband and wife to take the neighbor's discarded spoons and profit by selling them. Have them write a short opinion piece explaining their position. (I, WC)

Tomás and the Library Lady/Tomás y la señora de la biblioteca
Written by Pat Mora
Illustrated by Raul Colón
Dragonfly Books, 1997
Tomás Rivera Mexican American Children's Book Award,
A Common Core Exemplar Text

In this book based on the life of Tomás Rivera, we meet Tomás as a young boy who loves the stories his grandfather tells—but has heard them over and over. His life opens to a world of possibilities when Papá Grande introduces him to the library. This book represents every educator's wish list: that books open doors to learning, that we learn from each other, and that we respect one another's backgrounds and interests. It may be idealistic, but what's wrong with putting those ideas in students' minds as they become confident, capable readers and writers themselves?

Libraries. I couldn't love them more. But they are underfunded and under fire in many places. After reading this book as a group, ask students to discuss the role of the library in their lives and to create a poster campaign to use the library more—get a library card, bring in families, explore the rich collections and resources, and so on. (I, V)

Viva Frida
Written by Yuyi Morales
Photography by Tim O'Meara
Roaring Brook, 2014
Pura Belpré Award, Caldecott Honor Book

This bilingual text is a glorious visual feast for the eyes. The more you look, the more you see. Simple words and magnificent illustrations lead the reader through the piece. This biography of artist Frida Kahlo uses creativity, language, and art to inform the reader about her unusual life and background. The illustrations add imagination and style that reveal the multisensory theme in depth.

Examine each page in detail and note what the words prompt the reader to look for and respond to. Make a chart for each page spread and record the details of what students find in the illustrations that match the words. Then have students create a new page for the book and illustrate it with the details that would go along with it. (I, WC)

Ideas: Chapter Books as Mentor Texts

Dancing Home/Nacer bailando
Written by Alma Flor Ada and Gabriel M. Zubizarreta
Atheneum, 2013
Junior Library Guild Selection

"Well, you can teach the teachers," said Lupe. "After all, some of us have to learn a whole new language. I'm sure they can manage to learn to say our names. And the kids—you can do like Camille does and just laugh" (96).

If you have not already done so after reading about it in Chapter 1, now would be an excellent time to view the video that Alma Flor Ada and her son Gabriel M. Zubizarreta share on YouTube (see p. 6 for the URL). The book itself deals with the very real issues of immigration in the lives of Margie and Lupe. Each learns what "home" really means in this beautifully lyrical and insightful book.

After sharing the passage above, ask students to consider something they would like to teach teachers. What would make their learning lives easier and more positive if only the teacher had an insight into how they tick, what matters to them, and what helps them learn? Invite students to create an e-mail or blog post to teachers about their ideas, keeping them upbeat and helpful. And as a teacher, model this idea in an exchange in writing by telling students what matters to you in your teaching. Maybe there are things about you that students would like to know so they can relate to the goals you have for them as learners. (I, V)

Island Treasures
Written by Alma Flor Ada
Illustrations by Antonio Martorell and Edel Rodriguez
Atheneum, 2015

The first vendor to call out his wares each morning was the panadero, *the baker.*
> Pan . . . panadero . . . calentito . . .
> Pan de leche . . . pan de huevo . . . calentito
> *Fresh-baked bread . . . the baker's here . . .*
warm bread . . . milk bread . . . egg bread . . . still warm from the oven.
> *. . . The baker's bread came to us right from the oven. Sometimes we dipped it in* café con leche—*warm milk with a few drops of very strong coffee—or we covered it with butter and savored each small bite.*
> From *Days at La Quinta Simoni:* "Street Vendors' Voices," (98)

In a sensory collection of memoirs about growing up in Cuba, Alma Flor Ada creates imagery that is so fresh and alive, readers feel as if we are experiencing the same events; meeting people so well described, they feel like new friends; and getting insight into Cuban customs and life. It's a treasure trove of stories that have appeared in other publications, wrapped up as a gift to upper-elementary readers in this new book. The extensive Spanish-to-English glossary extends our understanding of the stories and their origins.

The preceding passage from "Street Vendors' Voices" is an example of Alma Flor Ada's ability to take readers deep into a moment and bring it to life with sensory details. She doesn't try to write about everything in this one passage, just describes the sounds, tastes, and smells of the morning. Ask students to think about their favorite breakfast or meal, then write about that one idea by drawing on all their senses: sight, touch, taste, smell, and feel. (I, WC)

Return to Sender/Devolver al remitente
Written by Julia Alvarez
Translated by Liliana Valenzuela
Yearling, 2009
Pura Belpré Award

Tonight at midnight, Mr. President, when it turns into the 16th of September, it will be our Fourth of July in Mexico. It is the date when our country first became independent . . .

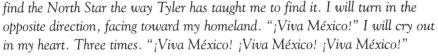

    Tonight, Mr. President, I am going to stay up until it is midnight. Then I will tiptoe through the trailer and come outside and lift my arms just above my shoulders to find the North Star the way Tyler has taught me to find it. I will turn in the opposite direction, facing toward my homeland. "¡Viva México!" I will cry out in my heart. Three times. "¡Viva México! ¡Viva México! ¡Viva México!"

    But because, as Mr. B says, we are all citizens of one planet, indivisible with liberty and justice for all, I will also turn toward where you live in your beautiful white house, Mr. President.

    "¡Viva los Estados Unidos del Mundo!" I will cry out to myself. "Long live the United States of the World! ¡Viva! ¡Viva! ¡Viva!" (71–72)

As a story from two points of view about immigration, this book is bound to challenge thinking about this emotionally charged and contemporary issue. It's the story of two loving families: Mari's family, who illegally immigrate to the United States in search of work, and Tyler's family, who struggle to keep their Vermont farm running after a tractor accident disables Tyler's father. A talented young writer who learns to express her deepest hopes and fears in words, Mari writes a poignant letter to the president of the United States about her plight and asks him to think about all children in a situation such as hers.

    Ask students to consider which traditions they would miss the most if they no longer lived in the United States of America. Ask them to compare their holidays and traditions with those of another country. Have them create a holidays and traditions chart and share what they discover with the class. (I, V)

WRITING 90 MILES
by Enrique Flores-Galbis

My second book, *90 Miles to Havana,* started out as a series of biographical sketches, initially based on pleasant memories of a privileged life, but as the writing continued, and I dug deeper, those sunny memories started to turn dark. You see, I was born in the year of the last scheduled presidential election in Cuba. One of the three candidates, Fulgencio Batista, did not like his odds of getting elected, so he decided to give a head fake to the Constitution and declare himself El Presidente. He took control (again) in a military coup, and then promptly canceled elections, alienating a large segment of the population and energizing the long-festering and violent opposition. My golden years in Havana, the time between Batista's coup and the Cuban Revolution, were a time of economic growth and escalating political unrest and violence. Our parents tried to shield us from the upheaval, but as the violence intensified, muffled gunfire and explosions in the distance eventually came roaring down our street to knock at our door.

When I handed in my first draft, my editor suggested that the book should start closer to when we left Cuba. After all, it was supposed to be about our departure with Operation Pedro Pan and the evacuation of 14,000 unaccompanied children to camps in southern Florida. But as I edited away the early chapters, I realized that I was leaving out my unique, child's point of view of a very important historical moment—a revolution in progress. It wasn't until I arrived in the United States that I realized just how strange it was for a ten-year-old to be thinking about political intimidation and fear, and seeing the parallels between dictators and bullies in the school yard. My new American friends were not thinking or worrying about those things. They had been born into a stable democracy with a constitution and laws that were generally respected. There were regular elections. People talked freely here and seemed to be able to come to an agreement without shouting or shooting at each other.

So I decided to change the book from personal memoir to historical fiction, a form that would allow me to include a broader range of experiences to tell a bigger story. I created a main character to whom readers could relate and whom they'd be willing to inhabit, and then dropped them into a kid-sized, playground revolution in the refugee camp. In this way I could share my insights into the workings of a revolution, the anatomy of bullies, and doing things the "democratic way," not by telling the readers about it, but by letting them experience it as they ride along with the main character.

As a writer I feel that my books are successful when they provide a magical means of transport from the reader's world into the life of another. If this new perspective creates empathy and understanding, I sleep soundly at night. ⑨

Chapter 3

THE METICULOUS PLANNER

ORGANIZATION

On the surface, the organization trait appears relatively straightforward. It's easy to understand why organization is important. After all, writing needs a beginning, middle, and end, with a liberal dose of key words and phrases to pull it all together. But don't let its seemingly simple exterior fool you—this is one tough trait to master. In fact, as many writers will tell you, it turns out to be one of the hardest to get right.

The organization trait is the internal structure of the piece—the thread of meaning, the pattern of logic. Organization would be the planner behind the scenes at our traits dinner party. Typical structures include point-by-point analysis, chronological play of events, deductive logic, cause and effect, comparison and contrast, problem and solution, and order of importance and complexity. The structure the writer chooses depends on his or her purpose for writing and the intended audience.

Writing that is well organized demonstrates logic and reason as it evolves from beginning to end. Events and details unfold in a way that intrigues readers and leads them through the ideas. Information is presented in the right doses and at the right moments, depending on the author's purpose and audience, so the reader never loses sight of the main idea. Transitions from one point to the next are clear. Well-organized writing usually wraps up with a sense of resolution and ties up loose ends. Sometimes, however, it leaves the reader with something to think about by posing bigger questions that invite further contemplation and study. To accomplish all this, the writing must skillfully and confidently apply the organization trait's key qualities:

- **Creating the Lead:** The beginning grabs the reader's attention and leads him or her into the piece naturally. The beginning entices the reader to keep reading, providing a tantalizing glimpse of what is to come.
- **Using Sequence and Transition Words:** The piece contains a variety of carefully selected sequence and transition words, which are placed wisely to guide the reader through the text by showing how ideas progress, relate, and/or diverge.
- **Structuring the Body:** The piece is easy to follow because the details fit together logically. The writer slows down to spotlight important points or events and speeds up when he or she needs to keep the reader moving along.
- **Ending with a Sense of Resolution:** The writer sums up his or her thinking in a natural, thoughtful, and convincing way and has anticipated and answered any lingering questions, giving the reader a strong sense of closure.

The Traits Dinner Party: Organization

Organization, a longtime pal of Ideas, offers help to prepare for the dinner party because he's got a real flair for pulling an event together. Organization, after all, has a knack for thinking through all the details ahead of time: no element is too small, and no aspect of the party is too trivial for his sharp-eyed attention. He busily sets the table, arranges the seating, and makes sure everything is ready at the right time for the meal to go off without a hitch. He's a type-A personality with a creative streak that helps him mix things up so they don't become predictable. He's a sharp dresser, with accessories meticulously coordinated, including the neon-pop sneakers peeking out from under his perfectly pressed pants. And *please*, don't ever ask where Organization bought the place-setting decorations or centerpieces! He'd never even consider buying something packaged or premade. He always lets the guest list and Ideas inspire his theme so the dinner is unique to the occasion, from appetizer through main course and dessert.

During dinner, Organization sits to the right of Ideas, supporting her in subtle but significant ways throughout the meal: checking that glasses remain full, courses are served while piping hot or still chilled, and each guest's plate is filled with favorites. And at the end of the evening, Organization's happy to let Ideas take credit for hosting such a fabulous party, because he knows his behind-the-scenes work planning and arranging made the whole event flow smoothly. He and Ideas sit back after all the other guests have gone home, clink glasses, and celebrate their successful evening.

Choosing Mentor Texts for the Organization Trait

Strong organization is invisible to the reader. Like a building's architectural structure, it supports and holds everything together—concrete, steel, and bricks and mortar—but we rarely see it. What we do see is the architect's finished idea for the structure: a bank, a school, an apartment building, a shopping complex, a restaurant, a car wash. Regardless of their purpose, each of them needs a sturdy foundation and structure—the equivalent of organization in writing. As every construction worker will tell you, it's hard yet crucial work to build a sturdy foundation.

Take heart. As students learn the purposes (modes) for writing, they gain a big leg up on the organization ladder. Writing unfolds differently, depending on its purpose. The modes of writing are:

Narrative Writing
>   Purpose: To tell a story
>   What the writer typically does:
>>   Offers a clear, well-developed story line
>>   Includes characters that grow and change over time
>>   Conveys time and setting effectively
>>   Presents a conflict and resolution
>>   Surprises, challenges, or entertains the reader

Informative/Explanatory Writing (Traditional term: Expository)
>   Purpose: To explain and provide information
>   What the writer typically does:
>>   Informs the reader about the topic
>>   Goes beyond the obvious to explain what is interesting
>>   or curious about the topic

Focuses on making the topic clear for the reader
Anticipates and answers the reader's questions
Includes details that add information, support key ideas,
and help the reader make personal connections

Opinion/Argument Writing (Traditional term: Persuasive)
Purpose: To construct an argument using reason and logic
What the writer typically does:
States a position clearly and sticks with it
Offers good, sound reasoning
Provides solid facts, opinions, and examples
Reveals weaknesses in other positions
Uses voice to add credibility and show confidence

That's not to say, however, that writing always stays neatly in one mode. You'll find examples of writing that cross purposes and mix modes, and you'll likely notice that the best-written books do this masterfully—they mingle modes even though there is a single overriding intent for the piece as a whole. With time and practice, you'll be able to spot the places in a narrative text, for example, where an opinion is expressed to further develop the character, or you'll find an anecdote perfectly placed in an informational piece to make the account more clear. By dipping in and out of different modes in a single piece of writing, the writer provides a textured and layered piece that presents the idea in multifaceted ways—making it possible for readers to engage with it at different levels.

Understanding the role of mode in writing is another issue to consider as you hunt for books and passages that can serve as mentor texts. In addition to looking for models that will help students see each key quality in action, you may want to identify passages by mode and discuss how they affect the text. If you are using mentor texts to show students how authors organize their ideas, for example, they need to understand that a story that is organized chronologically is quite different from informational text, even though the story may contain nuggets of information throughout. Here are some questions to help you dig into books and find organizational inspiration:

Creating the Lead: How does the book begin? How does a book on a similar topic begin? Which technique makes you want to keep reading? Are fiction leads different from nonfiction leads? What grabs kids and what doesn't when they begin to read a picture book, a chapter book, a section of a longer text?

Using Sequence Words and Transition Words: How do authors move through time? How do they link one idea to the next? How do they show how ideas are related to each other? What clues does the author provide about what will come next? How do they connect thinking without relying too much on the most obvious sequence words and transition words (first, second, finally, and so on)?

Structuring the Body: Is the writing easy to follow? Does the information fit where it is placed? Is the information or story line logically organized so it fleshes out the topic? Are like pieces of information found in the same paragraphs or sections? Has the author mingled modes to make the overall purpose and main idea clear?

Ending with a Sense of Resolution: Does the piece have a smart ending or is it fairly predictable? Does the ending give the topic closure? Are there things to think about more at the end? If the writer created a surprise ending, did he or she leave small, subtle clues in the body of the text about what was to come? Does the ending make you want to talk to someone about the book and its idea?

Beware of Formulas for Organization

Bad things happen when we rely too heavily on canned structures and formulas: a five-paragraph essay, a topic sentence and three supporting details, graphic organizers for every task, and so on. When we do these things, we take away the writer's need to think and problem-solve. Writing, after all, is a thinking skill. When we deprive students of this critical decision-making process, their writing doesn't fulfill its potential: the idea gets smothered in the predictable pattern of organization, and the reader dozes off. But even more important, the writer doesn't get a chance to flex his or her writing muscles and develop the skills to make smart organizational decisions on his or her own.

I know the argument: "I use structures only to scaffold student work. My kids really like the formula—it supports them when they are lost about how to order their writing. They can discard the structures once they learn how to write better." Fine—if the process truly worked that way. It doesn't. Kids wear formulas like life jackets, even when they are out of the water. After all, without an expected writing plan in hand, they would organize the writing on their own using logic and reasoning. Harder, yes. But so much better for the long-term ability of the student to develop and continue to improve. It's much easier to follow someone else's blueprint—no problem solving required. This is why I take issue with formulas. Kids stop thinking, and when we let them do that, we lose the momentum for the good if not great writing ahead. Imagine, if every city building followed the same architectural blueprint, how boring the skyline would be!

One more thing: writing formulas and recipes shoot too low. Our students are better writers, better thinkers than any canned approach allows them to demonstrate. They need a chance to see how the experts do it by reading many texts through the lens of the organization trait. They need teachers who can guide them through mentor texts so they can see the different patterns of logic authors apply and varied structures authors build. The ultimate goal is to fill students up with the possibilities so they internalize new thinking patterns and try out new writing structures for themselves. Our students should be the architects of their own writing. Mentor texts can provide the right scaffolding as they build.

Mentor Texts for the Organization Trait: Picture Books

A Is for Activist/A de activista
Written by Martha E. Gonzalez
Illustrated by Innosanto Nagara
Triangle Square Press, 2013

What an interesting topic for a board book! This book, intended for readers of every age, is rich with high-level vocabulary, pictures, rhymes, and progressive ideas. It clearly has its eye set on the next generation of politically active and environmentally conscious young people. Organized by letters of the alphabet, it makes an excellent model for writing ABC books on other topics as well.

Use the structure of *A Is for Activist* to point out the organization of the text and the fact that accurate and specific words must be used regardless of the medium—including a board book. Make a list of the words that stand out in the text, and note the rhythm and rhymes in the running text. Invite students to create alphabet books on causes or issues of their choice—topics that have meaning to them that can be conveyed through their voices. (O, WC)

Abuelo and the Three Bears/Abuelo y los tres osos
Written by Jerry Tello
Illustrated by Ana López Escrivá
Scholastic, 1997

A warm adaptation of *Goldilocks and the Three Bears*, this book weaves many Latino customs and traditions into the story line, which makes reading it fun. It's an upside-down book: Hold it one way and you can read the English version, but turn it around to read the story in Spanish.

Ask students to compare and contrast the similarities and differences between the two versions of the Goldilocks story. Have them make a chart of each example that shows different language choices and story adaptations. (O, WC)

Abuela's Weave
Written by Omar S. Castañada
Illustrated by Enrique O. Sanchez
Lee and Low Books, 1993
1993 Parents' Choice Award Winner

Weaving traditional Guatemalan tapestries and fabrics is a gift Esperanza's grandmother gladly shares with her granddaughter. As they prepare for market, however, Esperanza is concerned that her *abuela's* facial birthmark will make her the subject of ridicule and even feed rumors about her being a witch. At the market, customers flock to their pieces, and they quickly sell out—the quality of the work overcoming any concerns about Abuela's disfigurement. Told in English with a few Spanish words woven in, this is a story rich with culture, personal growth, and family pride.

This simply told narrative can be a mentor text for how to tell a story in a logical sequential order using sequence and transition words throughout. Help students break the story down by its segments and notice how the events are logically yet artfully tied together. (O, SF)

Book Fiesta! Celebrate Children's Day/Book Day/ Celebremos El dia de los niños/El dia de los libros
Written by Pat Mora
Illustrated by Rafael López
HarperCollins Children's Books, 2009

What a joyful book! From beginning to end, readers explore all the ways to celebrate *El día de los niños/El día de los libros*— Children's Day/Book Day, founded by the author and now celebrated through the American Library Association every year on April 30. Presented as a bilingual text, it asks, With whom will we read? Where shall we read? Where will our stories take us? The text takes readers on an energetic adventure through these questions to remind us about the importance of books.

Organize your own Book Day after reading this charming story. Ask students to help you plan the event and create invitations to other classes to join them in a celebration of reading and writing. Create a plan for Book Day and show the flow from the beginning of the day to the end with smooth transitions. (O, I)

¡Bravo!
Written by Ginger Foglesong Guy
Illustrated by René King Moreno
Greenwillow Books, 2010

A brother and sister go on a treasure hunt in this simple picture book that invites readers to join the search. Everyday objects such as bells, an umbrella, and a horn are discovered on the pages, linked by the words "¿Entonces? What next?" At the end, friendship and a celebration of marching, singing, and playing is endorsed by other family members: "¡Bravo!"

Using the inspiration from the book, ask students to create a list in English and Spanish of treasure hunt items that they find around the school. Tell them they will be creating a class book with these items that is organized the same way as the mentor text. Help them find the sequence words and transition words used in ¡Bravo! and create a list. Feel free to help students add additional sequence and transition words to the list as well. Use the list to connect the discovery of each object in an order that makes sense to create a group book modeled after ¡Bravo! Have students then organize and act out their celebration with marching, singing, and playing as shown in the mentor text. (O, WC)

Caye Boy: Barefoot Adventures of an Island Child
Written by Jessica Retsick Wigh
Illustrated by Andrew Young
CreateSpace, 2013

As the sun comes up, the reader gets a glimpse into the different adventures that "caye boy" and his little brother will have as they explore the island where they live. This simple story shows young writers how to write a narrative that covers a short amount of time and engages readers with everyday language that creates pictures in their minds of this delightful day. The book ends as the day ends, providing a nice sense of completion and resolution.

Have students notice where the story begins and where it ends. Create a storyboard of the key events so students can visualize how the story builds and then resolves. Ask them to think of one event that could have happened that can be added to the text and to write about it with simple yet appealing words; they can show, too, where their imagined event might be inserted into the story line. (O, WC)

Cecilia and Miguel Are Best Friends/Cecilia y Miguel son mejores amigos
Written by Diane Gonzales Bertrand
Illustrations by Thelma Muraida
Arte Público, 2014

A warm and intimate look into the lifelong friendship of Cecilia and Miguel is chronicled in this bilingual story. The repeating refrain "Cecilia and Miguel are best friends" opens every page, followed by words that describe different things they've done together and pictures that look like photos from a scrapbook. Each page focuses on the details of events that cement their bond over the years. The sweet conclusion to the book harkens back to the beginning, which should be noted and discussed as well.

Whether it is the time they broke a piñata together, when Miguel broke his leg but still took Cecilia to her *quinceañera*, when they separated to head to different parts of the country for college, or when their lives are reunited, this book shows how to organize an idea with many details so it is easy for the reader to follow using a repetitive refrain. It's an example of how ideas and organization work hand in hand. Students might enjoy writing their own ideas of small moments of friendship and adding them into the text using the same refrain so they fit naturally into the story. (O, I)

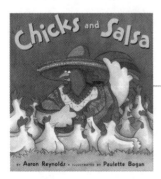

Chicks and Salsa
Written by Aaron Reynolds
Illustrated by Paulette Bogan
Bloomsbury, 2007

Publishers Weekly calls this book a "literary fandango"—I couldn't agree more. Aaron Reynolds is a master at writing snappy, smart text. The chickens in this narrative are sick and tired of chicken feed—and who can blame them? It's bland, boring, and tasteless. The rooster decides to help by showing the chickens how to make spicy, fresh salsa! The story really develops when the pigs start to grumble about their slop. The problem-solution structure of this story will be enjoyed by all.

Look closely at the ending of this book: clever Aaron Reynolds uses a French phrase to wrap it all up. Ask students why the author used a phrase that is not Spanish to send the signal to the reader that the book is over. Then have them examine the end pages that include the recipes for Quackamole and Rooster's Roasted Salsa. Ask kids to add a line to each recipe that wraps it up in an unpredictable way. (O, WC)

Counting on Community
Written and Illustrated by Innosanto Nagara
Triangle Square Press, 2015

I'm fascinated by this new genre of board books. Unlike their predecessors, these books are directed to an older audience who will appreciate the complexity of the ideas. *Counting on Community* focuses on positive changes that begin at the local level: planting a garden, helping a neighbor, picking up trash. Using a 1–10 organizational pattern, the reader comes away with ten ideas to improve neighborhood life.

Invite students to brainstorm a list of ideas to support and improve their local neighborhoods and arrange those ideas in order, 1–10, as modeled in the mentor text. Encourage them to revise and change words and phrases as their version of the book is assembled so there is rhythm and flow between ideas—and if possible, see if they can make some of them rhyme. (O, SF)

Dear Primo: A Letter to My Cousin
Written and Illustrated by Duncan Tonatiuh
Abrams Books for Young Readers, 2010

Charlie lives in the United States, and Carlitos lives in Mexico. Because they are cousins, they write each other letters describing their lives and what it's like growing up in two very different places. As they get to know each other better, the cousins realize they have a great deal in common, regardless of their geography, and Charlie and Carlitos vow to pay each other a visit.

Have students work in pairs to take the roles of Charlie and Carlitos and extend the story to explore what happens when they visit each other. Have students consider a new ending for the book that focuses on their first in-person interaction with each other. (O, I)

Elena's Serenade
Written by Campbell Geeslin
Illustrated by Ana Juan
Atheneum Books for Young Readers, 2004

Elena has big dreams of becoming a glassblower like her father. However, Elena is small, and she's a girl. Many people—including her father—tell her that she will never be able to do it. But Elena knows better. When the time comes, she creates masterful art pieces and proves her talents not only to those who scoffed at her but also to her most important critic, her father. This artful and inspiring book weaves many Spanish words throughout.

Students should think about one thing in life they'd really like to do. Ask them to make a T-chart and, on one side, write all the reasons they know they can acquire the skills they need to achieve their dream. On the other side, have them list all the obstacles between them and their dream. Tell students to summarize the information on the T-chart in a few sentences underneath it, focusing on how they will achieve or learn something new, no matter how many perceived obstacles may be in their way. (O, I)

¡Fiesta!
Written by Ginger Foglesong Guy
Illustrated by René King Moreno
Greenwillow Books, 2007

In this simple bilingual picture book, readers learn words in English and Spanish associated with a fiesta. Linked by the phrase "*¿Qué más?* What else?" the counting book explores all the goodies that will fill the piñata for the fiesta.

Ask students to think about what other fun things might be found at a fiesta, such as games, food, people, and music. Have them pick one and, with a small group, create a counting book in English and Spanish that would be associated with their choice. They can use the phrase "*¿Qué más?* What else?" to link each item. Or, allow them to explore other phrases in Spanish and/or English that might work just as well. (O, I)

Gathering the Sun: An Alphabet in Spanish and English

Written by Alma Flor Ada

English translation by Rosa Zubizarreta

Illustrated by Simón Silva

Rayo, 2001

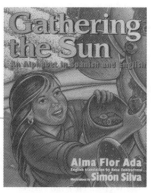

Here readers find bilingual poems that celebrate culture, family, history, and the gathering of the harvest. The poems are organized alphabetically and allow readers to see and feel what it's like to work the land and rejoice in the beauty and fruitfulness of what the earth provides. (On a personal note, this is the first book I read, years ago, that began my love affair with texts that celebrate Latino culture. Thank you, Alma Flor Ada.)

Use this book as a model for writing poems organized by the alphabet. Ask students to help decide on several new topics that go along with different letters of the alphabet and are inspired by the poems in *Gathering the Sun*. Then put them in groups to brainstorm and write poems on topics that go along with as many letters as possible. Have students share their poems with the large group at the end and post for all to enjoy. (O, V)

Gazpacho for Nacho

Written by Tracey Kyle

Illustrated by Carolina Farías

Two Lions: Amazon, 2014

Most parents will tell you their children got stuck on one food at some point in their early years. In this story, Nacho can't get enough gazpacho—he eats it morning, noon, and night. No other foods, no matter how delicious, can tempt him . . . until one day, he discovers firsthand the rich and tasty variety of vegetables at the market. Nacho realizes that he can come to love other foods that include vegetables as well. This charming rhyming story that includes Spanish words and a glossary also has a "Yummy-in-the-Tummy" gazpacho recipe.

Encourage students to create recipes of their own favorite foods, emphasizing the benefits of fresh vegetables and fruits and how "Yummy-in-the-Tummy" their favorite treat can be if they follow the directions carefully. (O, V)

Good Dream, Bad Dream: The World's Heroes Save the Night!/ Sueño bueno, sueño malo: Los heroes del mundo salvan la noche!
Written and Illustrated by Juan Calle and Serena Valentino
Immedium, 2014

Julio is sure the monsters in his dreams will conquer him until his father shares a special secret! Did you know that anyone has the power to summon mythical characters to battle dream demons? Readers find that the good dreams can prevail.

Brainstorm all the things that students think are scary: snakes, monsters under the bed, zombies, spiders, and so on. Then have them write out the way each monster can be conquered, as modeled in the book *Good Dream, Bad Dream*, providing a creative solution to every problem. (O, I)

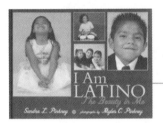

I Am Latino: The Beauty in Me
Written by Sandra L. Pinkney
Photographs by Myles C. Pinkney
Hachette Book Group, 2007

Beautiful, striking photographs of young Latino children will make you smile from the inside out in this informational picture book. Organized by the senses and the repeating phrase "Can you sense the beauty?," the book lets the reader explore the riches of food, music, language, and Latino culture with both English and Spanish words.

As you explore the book together, ask students to add more pages—more ideas for beauty, for the melody of the language, for the feeling of the music, for the strengths within every family, for the smell and taste of the foods—and to write a wonderful ending line, too. Ask students to determine where their pages fit into the organization of the book and insert the pages into it so that as readers enjoy the original text, they also see the writing of students. (O, I)

Just a Minute: A Trickster Tale and Counting Book
Written and Illustrated by Yuyi Morales
Chronicle Books, 2003
Pura Belpré Medal, Notable Books for a Global Society, Book Américas Award, Tomás Rivera Mexican American Children's Book Award

Grandma Beetle, in the trickster tradition, outsmarts Señor Calavera (a.k.a. Death) when he asks that she leave with him right away. Grandma Beetle stalls by counting out the details necessary to prepare for her birthday celebration. By the time she finishes her counting, Señor Calavera has gone, leaving her a note that he'll be back—next year.

Ask students to write a trickster tale using at least five reasons they could tell the teacher to stall taking a test. Let them use their imaginations to come up with fanciful excuses with the outcome they want: no test! (O, I)

Just in Case: A Trickster Tale and Spanish Alphabet Book
Written and Illustrated by Yuyi Morales
Roaring Brook, 2008
Pura Belpré Gold Medal Award for Illustrations, Pura Belpré Honor Book for Narrative, 2009 Bank Street—Best Children's Book of the Year

Yuyi Morales has written and illustrated an uproariously funny, fresh, and oh-so-clever story about finding the perfect birthday gift for Grandma Beetle's special day. Young readers will enjoy this romp through unusual gift options for each letter of the alphabet. This trickster tale sprinkled with Spanish words will be enjoyed over and over again.

Alphabet books provide an organizational structure for writing that students of all ages find engaging. Use this book as an example of how to be creative with structure, and ask kids to add rich vocabulary to alphabet books of their own. Allow them to choose the genre, too—from trickster stories like this one to informational texts on topics that intrigue them. (O, I, WC)

Kikirikí * Quiquiriquí
Written by Diane de Anda
Translated by Karina Hernandez
Illustrated by Daniel Lechón
Piñata Books, 2004

Celia and Marta realize the family just purchased a rooster that was not intended for a pet—and they are not happy about what might happen to him. They hide their new friend in their bedroom closet to protect him from his dreaded fate as dinner. Roosters crow at dawn, however, and that gives poor Kikirikí's location away. Many options are considered for what should happen next, and, with much persuasion and persistence, the girls are victorious in saving the rooster's life: he is sent to a farm to live a happy, long life.

Ask students to think about another animal, such as a turkey, chicken, cow, or pig, that might need intervention to be saved from being served on the dinner table.

They can create a short story following the organizational structure of *Kikirikí*, in which the options are considered and ultimately the best one is chosen to save the animal. (O, I)

Marisol McDonald and the Clash Bash/Marisol McDonald y la fiesta sin igual

Written by Monica Brown
Illustrated by Sara Palacios
Lee and Low Books, 2013

The best birthday wishes are not always for things, as readers find out in this sweet bilingual story. The high energy of this book makes it easy to enjoy the tale of Marisol and her clash-bash birthday fiesta. Marisol's spirit and individualism come through loud and clear—with a pleasant surprise for all at the end.

The ending of this book is a perfect wrap-up for the main idea. Ask students to explain the big idea of the book and what it means to be "mismatched." Go back into the text and show examples of how the author brings out the main theme. Then reread the ending and have students write their opinion of how the author wrapped up the book's big idea in the conclusion. Guide them to explain whether they think it was effective and if there was a surprise for them as the reader. (O, I)

My Tata's Remedies/Los remedios de mi tata
Written by Roni Capin Rivera-Ashford
Illustrated by Antonio Castro L.
Cinco Puntos, 2015
2015 Pura Belpré Illustrator Honor Award

Based on the traditions of the American Southwest, this is a book of natural and safe remedies for medical problems in everyday life: burns, sore spots, insect stings, a cold, an eye infection, and more. It's practical and gives readers many ways to care for themselves and others from ideas that have been passed down in the traditional home culture of Latino children.

Notice how the book is organized. Each page presents a situation that needs a solution along with a naturopathic remedy. Ask students to think of things that are done in their homes to help with everyday medical problems and then to write a passage to describe one. Put all the ideas together in a logical organizational pattern, perhaps grouped by body system or simply listed alphabetically, and add sequence and transition words to tie the pieces together into one booklet. Create a table of contents, title, and cover for the book. You might even want to send copies home for the families of each student. (O, I)

Rubia and the Three Osos
Written by Susan Middleton Elya
Illustrated by Melissa Sweet
Disney-Hyperion Books, 2010

A new, updated twist on the familiar tale *Goldilocks and the Three Bears*, this story delights readers from page 1, when Mama Oso decides she needs to go on a walk as part of her South Woods diet plan to get thinner. Filled to the brim with Spanish words, this story has wonderful rhythm and energy. And a surprise ending!

Compare the ending of the original Goldilocks story with the ending of *Rubia and the Three Osos*. Ask students which they think is the more powerful ending. Then have them look at other fairy tales to see more examples of how the stories are wrapped up. Have them pick a new fairy tale and, with a partner, write a different ending that gives readers a surprise. (O, SF)

Tamalitos: A Cooking Poem/Un poema para cocinar
Written by Jorge Argueta
Illustrated by Domi
Groundwood Books, 2013

By carefully following every step in this story, readers will enjoy a mouthwatering cooking and eating experience. The brother and sister in this bilingual book have a great time showing us how to make *tamalitos* (little tamales), a traditional Peruvian dish made by steaming corn masa, cheese, and other ingredients in corn husks. The colorful recipe creates a full sensory experience, painting vivid images of how tasty tamalitos are going to be. On other pages, readers understand how important plants, earth, and sunlight are to creating the ingredients necessary for the yummy dish.

Ask students to brainstorm their favorite dishes and think about what the recipe might be for each one. Have pairs of children write out the ingredients and instructions for their recipes by following the format of the book—highly visual and verbally descriptive of taste, sounds, and smells. (O, WC, I)

Waiting for the Biblioburro
Written by Monica Brown
Illustrated by John Parra
Tricycle, 2011

Provide students with background about bookmobiles and movable libraries that come into local communities for easier access to books and library resources. Then share this story of Anna, who waits every day for the Biblioburro, a library collection carried on the back of a *burro*, to bring her new stories and books she can read and enjoy. In love with reading and writing, Anna creates her own story to share with the other children who wait eagerly for the Biblioburro to arrive in their town, too. In addition to an excellent beginning, there is strong use of sequence and transition words in this book; point this out to readers on a second reading.

Reread the beginning of the book and note the style: time setting, character, and action. Ask students to write the setting and name a character for another story using the technique modeled in *Waiting for the Biblioburro*. Explain that their introductions should be attention grabbing and provide enough information so that the reader can't wait to turn the page. (O, I)

Mentor Texts for the Organization Trait: Chapter Books

Baila, Nana, baila/Dance, Nana, Dance
Retold by Joe Hayes
Illustrated by Mauricio Trenard Sayago
Cinco Puntos, 2008
Aesop Prize

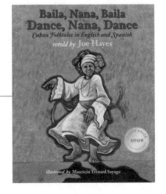

One year a young wife and her young husband harvested a big pile of yams from their field. Yams, rice, beans and an occasional chicken were just about all they ever had to eat, so they were very pleased. They had enough tasty yams to keep them supplied for the rest of the year. They piled the yams in a dry place under their house.

But that very afternoon, Jicotea, the tricky old turtle, crawled under the house to escape the hot sun and discovered the pile of yams.

"Here's food and shelter all together in a nice, cool place," Jicotea said to herself, and she burrowed deep into the pile of yams. "I may just spend the rest of my life right here." (11)

This bilingual book contains a series of tales from Cuba full of warmth and laugher—with a little magic and lots of wisdom thrown in, too. It's a rich collection that includes notes to the reader at the end of the book about the origin of each story and its significance. The passage above is excerpted from "Yams Don't Talk," an excellent example for beginning storytellers about how to start a folktale and structure it.

Discuss how the characters, setting, and problem are revealed right from the start in "Yams Don't Talk." Have students predict where the story will go, based on the beginning paragraphs. Then read the story aloud to them and compare what they thought to how it actually develops. Ask students to think of a different problem, new characters (be sure to include a trickster), and a new setting, and to write the opening paragraph of a story that sets up a tale that they can write in more detail as time allows. (O, I)

The Day It Snowed Tortillas/El día que nevaron tortillas

Folktales Told in Spanish and English by Joe Hayes
Illustrations by Antonio Castro L.
Cinco Puntos, 2003

Ending of "The Day It Snowed Tortillas":
> *From that day on, it didn't really matter whether the man was well educated or clever. It didn't matter if he was a good woodcutter. He was a rich man! He and his wife had three sacks of gold all to themselves. And the robbers never came back.* (8)

Ending of "The Cricket":
> *From that day on, it didn't matter how hard The Cricket tried to tell people that he wasn't a seer and had no special powers at all, no one believed him.* (42)

Ending of "Little Gold Star":
> *And from that day on, everyone called that girl* Cuerno Verde—*Green Horn!* (82)

In this bilingual collection of magical tales, author Joe Hayes takes readers on ten different adventures, from "The Day It Snowed Tortillas" to "The Prince." At the end, there are notes for readers about the idea and significance of each story. For students just learning about folktales, this is an ideal introductory collection to understand endings and how to wrap up folktales, since there are so many examples that show a predictable style.

Each tale's ending follows a similar pattern: the moral and a wrap-up. Read aloud the story endings above, and ask students how the endings are alike in this collection.

Then have students alter this traditional folktale pattern by writing new endings that are not as predictable or formulaic. Tell them to leave the reader with a sense of closure in a lively, fresh, and original way that includes a moral. (O, I)

VOICES BEYOND THE HORIZON
By F. Isabel Campoy

If 84 percent of teachers in our schools are white women, we need for their voices to listen to ours. That happens only through the power of excellent storytelling—and allies. Although it is still true that fewer than 2 percent of books published in the United States (1.7 percent to be exact) are written by Latino writers, we could build a list of thousands of wonderful texts written about the Latino culture by first-rate Latino authors, published in the twenty countries that constitute the Hispanic world. If the readers were bilingual, they could read them in the original language. If they weren't, let's face it, a translation would be a step forward, if there was a willing publisher. To do that we only need to look beyond our horizon.

As true believers in transformation, my coauthor Alma Flor Ada and I wrote *Yes! We Are Latinos* to honor the stories of friends and students, neighbors and family members who have been reflected in the thirteen poetic profiles that constitute 50 percent of that text. The other 50 percent provides a historical background to the roots of the specific character in each chapter. We know how necessary it is to read history from more than one source and more than one opinion. We are providing the fruits of our research in those essays.

Because I was born under a fascist dictatorship, my access to books was very limited and content from anywhere outside our borders practically impossible. I believed that what I read was actually the reality of the world—until a scholarship brought me to Trenton, Michigan, when I was sixteen. Since then I have traveled nonstop, through books, trains, and planes, and I know for sure, that is one way to educate for a global, anti-bias society.

Thank you to all the allies who are working toward an understanding and enjoyment of life on this tiny planet: Earth. ◉

Chapter 4

THE ENERGIZER

VOICE

Without a doubt, voice is the trait that makes teachers scrunch up their faces and sigh . . . deeply. It is the quality of writing that is undeniably important but oh-so-hard to quantify and describe. It may not be as tangible as other traits, but the effect of voice in writing can make or break a piece. Donald Murray frequently referred to voice as a primary quality of writing—the successful outcome of all the other traits working together at capacity. To achieve voice in writing there must be engagement with the topic, seamless organization, words and phrases that enliven the text, flowing sentences that draw readers in deeply, and yes—even conventions can and should add to the voice of the writing. As it turns out, voice is every trait's best friend. Voice brings energy to the dinner party, adds essence to the conversation.

And yet, we have a tough time teaching this trait. Maybe it's because we think it has to be taught like the other traits, when it's really more of a cumulative effect. Maybe it's because we had teachers who didn't emphasize how critical it is to connect with the reader. Maybe it's because our curriculums don't include the intentional development of voice as a key to writing success. As readers, however, we know it when a writer's voice permeates the writing—and we also know when it doesn't. And we far prefer reading writing that is alive with the energy, passion, and conviction of the writer's voice.

Voice is the tone and tenor of the piece—the personal stamp of the writer, achieved through a strong understanding of purpose and audience. It's the force behind the words that proves a real person is speaking and cares about what is being said. Voice helps convey the writer's point of view, too. Writers show a solid handle on why and for whom they're writing the piece, and choose an appropriate voice—cheerful or melancholy, humorous or serious, confident or uncertain, confrontational or conciliatory, fanciful or authoritative, and so on—to connect with and fully engage that reader.

Voice is the heart and soul of the writing—its very life. When writers are dedicated to their topics, they apply voice almost automatically because they are passionate about what they are saying and how they are saying it. They inject a flavor that is unmistakably their own and that distinguishes them from all other writers. To convey strong voice, writers must apply its key qualities with skill and confidence:

- **Establishing a Tone:** The piece shows how much the writer cares about the topic. The writing is expressive and compelling. The reader feels the writer's conviction, authority, and integrity.
- **Conveying the Purpose:** The reason for the writing is clear. The writer offers a point of view that is appropriate for the mode (narrative, informational, or opinion), which adds interest and compels the reader to read on.
- **Creating a Connection to the Audience:** There is a strong inter-action between the reader and the writer. The writer has considered what the reader needs to know and the best way to convey it by sharing his or her fascination, feelings, and opinions about the topic.
- **Taking Risks to Create Voice:** The writer expresses ideas in new ways, which makes the piece interesting, original, and fresh. The writing sounds like the writer because there are distinctive, just-right words and phrases that convey the intent of the writing.

The Traits Dinner Party: Voice

Voice sweeps through the door and greets the other traits like old friends she hasn't seen in ages. She embraces each guest warmly and takes her place next to Ideas at the head of the table, with her dear colleague Word Choice on her left. She makes small, insightful observations about the other traits as they wait for the meal to be served: a new hairstyle, a distinctive tie, a sparkling necklace and matching bracelet, a whiff of fragrance reminiscent of her winter garden. The other guests smile back in amusement at what Voice is wearing: a stylish bohemian frock of multicolored and multitextured fabrics accented with lace, buttons, and a ruffled asymmetrical hemline, along with lace-up boots. She plays with a long strand of pearls that hangs around her neck as she talks. The last time they were all together at a book award event, Voice was dressed quite formally, and the other traits note this head-to-toe makeover. But Voice always dresses for the occasion; this dinner party is stylish yet casual.

Voice is first to comment on the food's taste and texture, along with the aroma and presentation that make it so appealing and distinctive. She has a way of speaking that draws people toward her, an ability to put her own unique spin on an anecdote or a creative punch line on a joke. Voice asks fascinating questions about things that pique her curiosity. Her enthusiasm is infectious. Before the night is over, all the dinner guests are caught up in her effervescent spirit as she adroitly steers conversation between charming small talk and hilarious stories, to sober and contemplative observations, then back to light banter over dessert.

Choosing Mentor Texts for the Voice Trait

When you say to yourself while reading, *I wonder how that works or how that could happen* or, *I had no idea . . . . Where can I find out more?* When you laugh out loud, feel a deep sense of empathy, or think, *Oh my! That's amazing.* When the writing prickles the hair on the back of your neck—that's voice. Maya Angelou is widely quoted as saying, "The idea is to write so that people hear it and it slides through the brain and goes straight to the heart." Yes!

When choosing mentor texts for students to understand and embrace the urgency of adding their own voices to writing, think about the range of voices to explore. Happy and sad are what students think of first, but press them to go further and deeper into this trait by exploring how writers create texts that are hilarious or poignant—and teach them those words at the same time. Show them the books that evoke strong emotional responses and those that connect for other reasons: conviction, integrity, and authenticity. Here are some questions to consider as you look for books that illustrate the power of voice in writing:

Establishing a Tone: What is the overall feeling and tenor of this piece? (Think about whether it is thrilling, fun loving, knowledgeable, scary, wise, convincing, and so on.) Does it maintain that tone throughout or does it shift in places to provide variety? Does the author care about the topic? How does that come through to the reader? Is the writing expressive?

Conveying the Purpose: Is the overall purpose of the writing clear? Does it tell a story, inform, explain, or persuade? Does the author have a clear point of view? How does he or she make the purpose for the writing transparent for the reader? Is the voice credible?

Creating a Connection to the Audience: Where do you find yourself drawn in to the writing and nodding in agreement or shaking your head in wonder? What places stick in your mind after the reading is over? Is this a book about which you'd say to someone else, "You have to read this!" Do you imagine the author speaking even as you read the passage silently?

Taking Risks to Create Voice: Is this piece fresh and original? Has the author tried something new that stands out? Have you read a book on this topic before? How is this piece different? Are there places in the book where you think, *Oh, I didn't see that coming!* or, *I never thought about this topic that way.*

Voice Is Energy and Expression

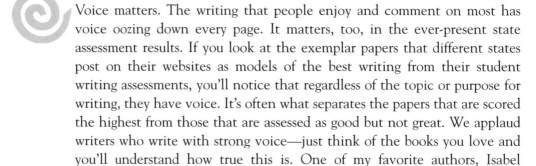

Voice matters. The writing that people enjoy and comment on most has voice oozing down every page. It matters, too, in the ever-present state assessment results. If you look at the exemplar papers that different states post on their websites as models of the best writing from their student writing assessments, you'll notice that regardless of the topic or purpose for writing, they have voice. It's often what separates the papers that are scored the highest from those that are assessed as good but not great. We applaud writers who write with strong voice—just think of the books you love and you'll understand how true this is. One of my favorite authors, Isabel Allende, has been quoted as saying, "That is the best part of writing: finding the hidden treasures, giving sparkle to worn out events, invigorating the tired soul with imagination, creating some kind of truth with many lies." That is how I envision voice.

Voice cannot be defined simply as personality. Writers have many personalities, depending on the purpose for writing. Everyone does. Let's be honest: my voice when I'm on the phone with the evil cable company is completely different from when I'm talking with a dear friend. But I use voice in both circumstances. And the voices (frustrated and annoyed versus delighted and upbeat) are used to convey the message as clearly as possible. Voice takes on different qualities, depending on its purpose, so it's confusing to students to define it simply as the writer's personality on the page. And a bit misleading, too.

Try this instead: Voice is energy. There should be energy in the words and phrases that help the reader engage with the writer's idea and connect to the message. Energy in a narrative piece, for instance, takes on a different form from that in an informational text, but each should be wired with language that gives the writing energy. Writing should be lively and engaging, regardless of the purpose. Otherwise, we get stacks and stacks of papers that are difficult to read and respond to because you really have no response as a reader. There is no life force, no sense of purpose, no reason for writing except it was assigned. Those papers—and we've all seen way too many of them—are deadly.

As you read aloud to students and notice them leaning in to catch every word—that's the writer's voice coming through loud and clear. Stop and mention it. Not on the first reading, of course. During the first reading you savor the book as a whole. But on a second, third, or fourth reading, ask students where they connected the most with the author's idea and look carefully at the writing craft that created that energy-filled moment.

And of course, when you read aloud different books and short pieces and students cry out, "Don't stop! Please keep reading" when it comes time to close the book and put it away—that's often because of voice. Name it. When students want to know more about why, and how, and what else, it's because the author has used his or her authentic voice to get them fascinated by the topic. Voice is the magic spell a writer casts over readers that we just don't want to break. I've felt that way; haven't you? When you read far too late into the night, just one more chapter, one more page, one more . . . that's voice.

Mentor Texts for the Voice Trait: Picture Books

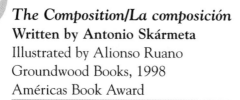

The Composition/La composición
Written by Antonio Skármeta
Illustrated by Alionso Ruano
Groundwood Books, 1998
Américas Book Award

Young Pedro is forced to choose between loyalty to his family and loyalty to his country's dictatorship. The government gets wind of an insurrection and uses schoolchildren to find out who is behind it by having students write a composition about what their parents do at night. Originally published in Spanish and set in a South American country, this thought-provoking children's book, although fiction, is bound to create discussion about different forms of government.

The contrast between Pedro's feelings about his family and his feelings about the government is pronounced. Read the pages where Pedro feels proud and happy followed by the pages where he fears what the government is doing. Discuss the tones and techniques the author uses to create voice to express those differences. Ask students to write a voice-filled letter to Pedro about his decision to lie, focusing on whether they agree or disagree with it. (V, I)

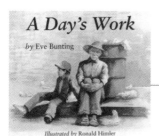

A Day's Work
Written by Eve Bunting
Illustrated by Ronald Himler
Clarion Books, 1994

Some of life's lessons cannot be told; they must be lived. Here readers explore a touching story of youth, age, and the integrity of an honest day's work. The narrator explores two different points of view: Francisco's and his grandfather's. Bunting is a master at taking difficult concepts and conceptualizing them for younger readers so they understand the complexities of challenging issues.

Ask students to write a page of dialogue between Francisco and his grandfather as if the story continued to the next day's events. Have students explain how Francisco would describe his feelings about going back to make right what he had wronged. They should use words that help the reader feel as deeply as the character does. (V, WC)

The Dead Family Diaz
Written by P. J. Bracegirdle
Illustrated by Poly Bernatene
Dial Books for Young Readers, 2012

The traditional celebration of the Day of the Dead takes a twist in this clever book that is told from the point of view of Angelito, a boy skeleton in the Land of the Dead who is terrified of running into living, breathing boys and girls. Loaded with kid appeal and funny situations, lively language, and vivid illustrations, this book is bound to become a classroom favorite—Addams Family–style.

Taking a familiar story and telling it from another point of view is an excellent way to add voice to writing. Ask students to identify the main characters and what they know about each one, using the dialogue as a cue. Challenge them to write a sequel to this story from the point of view of the living who meet up again next year at the Day of the Dead celebration. (V, SF)

Diego
By Jeanette Winter and Jonah Winter
Translated from English by Amy Prince
Dragonfly Books, 1991
New York Times Best Children's Book Award

This bilingual picture book features the life of the artist Diego, from a beginning that almost ended tragically through his travels around the world. Diego's journey through life moved him to paint his now-famous murals that represent his deep pride in his Mexican heritage. The combination of words and art in this book make it an excellent model to help students understand the role of art to inform and clarify the artist's and writer's intent.

Show students pictures of Diego's murals found on the Internet or in art books from the library. Ask students to describe one of the paintings and explain whether they think the painting has voice or not. Be sure to ask them to clearly explain the reasons for their responses using references to the painting itself. (V, WC)

I Dreamt . . . A Book About Hope
Written by Gabriela Olmos
Illustrated by Manuel Monroy et al.
Translated into English by Elisa Amado
Groundwood Books, 2013

A world without violence, fear, crime, and war . . . a dream for every child, no matter where they live. Every page of this moving and poignant book, which focuses on hope for reversing violent, negative situations, contains an artistic gift from one of Mexico's best artists. However, it is best for readers age eight or older, because some of the illustrations are disturbingly honest.

Challenge students to consider problems in today's world—or in their own lives—that they want to solve, then ask them to write a simple line as Gabriela Olmos has. Ask them also to examine the illustrations in *I Dreamt . . . A Book About Hope* and pick a style that best conveys the voice of their idea; they can explain their choice in writing or conversationally. If time allows, have students write a message to the illustrator of their choice and commend them on their work. (V, I)

La Mariposa
Written by Francisco Jiménez
Illustrated by Simón Silva
Houghton Mifflin, 1994

La Mariposa is the story of a young bilingual child who struggles but ultimately survives his first year in a new school. Readers will connect to the authentic voice, which is enhanced by the Spanish words woven in throughout. This story is a heartwarming, respectful attempt to educate all of us about how critical it is to nurture students through language.

Have students tell the story of a time when they were brand-new at something. Was it when they were learning a skill such as roller skating? Or perhaps they traveled to another country and tried a different language. Ask students to write the story so readers know exactly how they felt during that time. (V, WC)

Maria Had a Little Llama/Maria tenía una llamita
Written and illustrated by Angela Dominguez
Henry Holt, 2013
Pura Belpré Honor Book—Illustration Honor

Most of us know the simple rhyme version of "Mary Had a Little Lamb"—it's been around for a long time. In this charming retelling, readers read more about Maria and her mischievous little llama. This simple bilingual narrative features award-winning Peruvian illustrations and is bound to be a book students enjoy reading over and over again.

Challenge students to think of another simple rhyme such as "London Bridge Is Falling Down," "Humpty Dumpty Sat on a Wall," "Baa Baa Black Sheep" or "Jack and Jill Went Up the Hill" and create their own cultural retellings with some new twists. Keep the retellings simple, like the original, but add a different voice and fresh ideas. (V, I)

Niño Wrestles the World
Written and Illustrated by Yuyi Morales
Roaring Brook, 2013
Pura Belpré Award

Without question, this may be one of the most creative and energetic texts on this list. Niño uses all sorts of tactics to wrestle the most treacherous villains from Latino lore: la Momia de Guanajuato, La Llorona, el Etraterrestre, El Chamuco, and others. He never gives up; no challenge is too great for Niño. Readers will relate to his self-assurance and faith to take down opponents in single moves. Niño personifies confidence!

Ask students to note the way each of the challengers are described in the end papers of the book. Note how exuberantly and creatively each of the challengers is depicted. Ask kids to create a new challenger, name him or her, and describe their new character using the style and energy modeled in *Niño Wrestles the World*. (V, WC)

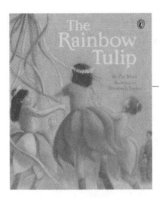

The Rainbow Tulip
Written by Pat Mora
Illustrated by Elizabeth Sayles
Puffin Books, 2003

Pat Mora writes in this book based on her mother's life about diversity and finding a way to celebrate her culture while trying to fit into a world with celebrations and customs that are different from any she's experienced before. In this English text that contains Spanish words and phrases, Stella insists on having a tulip costume for the Maypole dance and parade at her school—and though fearful she will be mocked for her choice, she ultimately finds her voice and takes big steps toward the acceptance she seeks.

Relate an example from your own life when you felt different from everyone else: because of your hobbies and interests, religion, geography, personal style, and so on. List the emotions associated with this experience: nervousness, concern, worry, excitement—as many as possible. Then ask students to write about a memory of their own and try to capture the feelings using words and images that help the reader connect with how they felt. (V, WC)

Mentor Texts for the Voice Trait: Chapter Books

Any Small Goodness: A Novel of the Barrio
Written by Tony Johnston
Illustrations by Raúl Colón
Scholastic, 2001

Really, my name was Arturo. Here's why: Three years ago our family came up from Mexico to L.A. . . . .

ANYWAY, first day of school, Miss Pringle, all chipper and bearing a rubbery-dolphin smile, says, "Class, this is Arthur Rodriguez." Probably to make things easier on herself. Without asking. Ya estuvo. Like a used-up word on the chalkboard, Arturo's erased.

Who cares? Not me. With such a name as Arthur, I'll fit in this school real well. Like a pair of chewed-up Nikes. Not stiff and stumbling new. American names are cool. Frank. Mike. Jake. They sound sharp as nails shot from guns.

I'm not the only one who's been gringo-ized. There's Jaime and Alicia and Raúl. Presto change-o! With one breath of teacher-magic, they're James and Alice and Ralph." (8–10)

Any Small Goodness features vignettes that compare and contrast American and Mexican cultures in different ways, emphasizing how it feels to be an immigrant trying to feel comfortable in a new place. This passage highlights how it feels to have your name changed without so much as a consultation. Note its personal voice and the use of similes.

Have students look up the origin of their name on the Internet and search to see if there is a version of it in another language. Ask students to imagine how their names would be changed if they were to move to another country such as Italy, China, South Africa, Russia, and so on. Have them write about what they discover and focus on the emotional attachment they have to their name and the feelings they'd have if someone changed it without asking. Point out examples of how Arturo's voice shines through, and invite kids to add their own spark of energy to their writing. (V, WC)

The Honey Jar
Written by Rigoberta Menchú, with Dante Liano
Illustrated by Domi
Groundwood Books, 2006

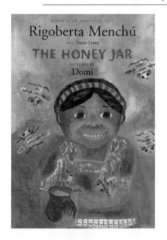

"I give you my word of honor as a weasel," she said. "You will find corn under the pek *rock."*

The people still had their doubts. So the weasel said, "Fine, I'll go with you and show you where the corn is hidden."

The villagers organized a huge procession and they carried all kinds of flowers—red geraniums, fire-colored bougainvillea, so many flowers that the people couldn't even be seen beneath them. They were like columns of army ants carrying food. And they carried their ocote *torches and banged on their drums. The sharp notes from their flutes floated in the midst of the sweet smelling flowers. It was amazing to see the villagers marching behind the weasel.* (Excerpt from "The Story of the Weasel Who Helped People Find Corn," p. 40)

Written by Rigoberta Menchú, a Nobel Peace Prize winner and Mayan activist, with the assistance of Dante Liano and enhanced with full-color artwork by Domi, *The Honey Jar* is an entertaining collection of short stories and tales derived from the author's childhood growing up in a Mayan culture. It's likely students will chuckle at the idea that the weasel in the passage above is so easily trusted, because weasels tend to symbolize trickster characters. And it's just as likely they will want to read the rest of the book for more voice-rich stories.

Review the passage with students and ask where they connect to the voice of the writer and what techniques were used—phrases that use color, for instance, or references to sounds. Discuss how the use of sensory details helps readers engage with the author's voice and feel the energy of the writing.

Ask students to write a visual passage about a scene at the local farmers' market, the cafeteria at school, a sporting event, or another place where many people are gathered. Remind them to help the reader connect with the idea by including words and phrases that are specific and colorful. (V, WC, SF)

The House on Mango Street/La casa en Mango Street
Written by Sandra Cisneros
Random House, 1984
American Book Award

Nenny and I don't look like sisters . . . not right away. Not the way you can tell with Rachel and Lucy who have the same fat popsicle lips like everybody else in their family. But me and Nenny, we are more alike than you would know. Our laughter for example. Not the shy ice cream bells' giggle of Rachel and Lucy's family, but all of a sudden and surprised like a pile of dishes breaking. And other things I can't explain. (17)

A classic. A rare and beautiful treasure that I hold dear to my heart, *The House on Mango Street* has mature themes that will not be right for every reader. But, if you pick and choose, you'll find chapters and vignettes that will fill students with images and language that will burrow deep into their writing marrow. You'll want readers to dip in and out of the text, available in English and Spanish, mining it for exquisite word choice and voice—and all the other traits as well.

When you focus on the passage above, ask students to work together to respectfully describe all the different types of laughs that they notice of friends, family, and peers (not by name!). Have them make a list and show them how Cisneros uses similes and metaphors to create the rich sounds and images throughout this chapter. Then have small groups or pairs of students come up with a description that uses figurative language to paint a picture in the reader's mind of one type of laugh. Share all the descriptions with the class and note the use of well-crafted language in each. (V, WC)

How Tía Lola Came to ~~Visit~~ Stay/De cómo Tía Lola vino ~~de visita~~ a quedarse
Written by Julia Alvarez
Translated by Liliana Valenzuela
Random House Children's Books, 2001

"Load-limit-one-ton," Tía Lola coos, hugging the girls, whose round faces turn pink. "Slippery-when-wet-proceed-with-caution." Mrs. Prouty looks perplexed. Especially when Tía Loa throws her arms around her, too.

"Awesome-get-a-life-chill-out," Tía Loa chants. Miguel cringes. He has been teaching Tía Loa some slang expressions in order to make her sound a little more cool in English. (63–64)

Miguel and his younger sister, Juanita, just moved from New York City to an old farmhouse in Vermont after their parents' divorce. It does not feel like home to them, and the adjustment is not easy, especially because their mother works long days. Help arrives with Tía Lola, their aunt from the Dominican Republic, who moves in and teaches and entertains the kids in her own unique style. Though they are skeptical at first, her magical character wins them over, and they beg her to stay. The English and Spanish versions address the issue of how to bridge two cultures.

Tía Lola's experience learning new English words is funny and touching at the same time. Ask students to think about the ten slang phrases in English that would be most helpful for someone learning the language, and write them down. Then, drawing upon the languages of all students in the class, create a list of everyday slang phrases in each language and compare and contrast their choices with the ones in English. (V, WC)

My Name Is Maria Isabel/Me llamo María Isabel
Written by Alma Flor Ada
Illustrations by K. Dyble Thompson
Atheneum, 1995

As she cut out bells and stars for decorations, María Isabel daydreamed about being a famous singer. Someday she would sing in front of a large audience, and her teacher would feel guilty that she had not let María Isabel sing in the Winter Pageant.

But later María Isabel thought, My teacher isn't so bad. It's all a big misunderstanding . . . If only there was some way I could let her know. Even if I'm not a

*great singer someday, it doesn't matter. All I really want is to be myself and not
make the teacher angry all the time. I just want to be in the play and to be called
María Isabel Salazar López.* (42)

María Isabel Salazar López is the new student, and her teacher dismisses her correct
name in favor of an English one, Mary. But María Isabel was named for beloved family
members, and that connection to them is part of her identity. Through the books she
loves to read, especially the one the librarian gave her, *Charlotte's Web*, she sorts out
some of the problems she is facing and also figures out what to write for her essay "My
Greatest Wish."

Ask students to tell the story of how they were named. Encourage them to talk to
family members to research the details. Have students write about their names,
including details about who named them, the name's significance, and the specific reasons why it was chosen. Tell them to write using energy similar to that conveyed in this
story: lively, personal, warm, humorous—whatever voice is appropriate to their own
writing. Ask students to add their own reactions to their names. For instance, if a student doesn't like her name, what would she change it to and why? (V, O, WC)

Under the Royal Palms/Bajo las palmas reales
Written by Alma Flor Ada
Atheneum, 1998

*As the days went by, school became bearable only
because as soon as the long-awaited bell rang, I would
run and cling to the window of the ballet school, imagining myself in the soft slippers, changing positions,
second, third, fourth, performing a jeté or a plié.*

    *One afternoon, the pale teacher disappeared from
view, and before I realized what was happening, she was
standing on the sidewalk by my side. "Do you want to
study ballet? What is your name?"*

Her voice was as soft as her gaze. "Come in," she said. "Come in."

    *Once she knew who I was, she called my mother and offered to accept me
in her class. My life was changed, not only after school but in school, too!*

    *I was never again bothered by prepositions and conjunctions, nor by my
inability to remember how much is seven times eight . . .* (54–55)

The warmth and wonder of her childhood days growing up in Cuba shine through on
every page in this collection of memoirs by celebrated author Alma Flor Ada. Readers
come to appreciate the big events and small happenings that shaped her character and
love of language during the 1940s, and I hope students will enjoy a glimpse inside life
on this beautiful island country.

In one story, "Gilda," the author reveals that she transferred from an American-style school with a strong emphasis on the arts to a Cuban one that focused primarily on memorization of facts and terms. "There was only one thing that allowed me to survive that horrible school with its treeless cement year—a school without songs, without drawing, without stories, without friends" (54). Read the passage aloud about music and dance and ask students to write a short piece on where they feel most connected to learning at school or at home. Tell them to think about the subjects they study—and don't study—and explain what makes learning meaningful and enjoyable for them. (V, I)

Yes! We Are Latinos/¡Sí! Somos Latinos
Written by Alma Flor Ada and F. Isabel Campoy
Illustrated by David Diaz
Charlesbridge, 2013
A Junior Library Guild Selection

"Where did you find it?"
Abuelita asks, looking at the book I am reading.
"It was on the top shelf.
Is this your diary, Abu Amaya?"
"That diary was written with tears.
My father wrote it for your mother and your uncles.
'Because they need to know,' he said. Now it is yours."

I'm glad it's Saturday, because
I can't stop reading.
This is my great-grandfather's diary,
But it is also my story—
The story that explains why I was born in Boston
And also who I am.
It seems like I've always known
Some of the facts—
but they become so real in his own voice. (64–65)

This compilation of thirteen vignettes showcases narrative poems with accompanying informational text that provides insight into history, culture, and the many different Latino and Latina voices living in the United States. Available in an English and Spanish version, the book is a rich collection of perspectives that provides beautifully written insights into the young Latino's search for identity in today's world.

The selected passage is an example of the poetic language and powerful messages found on every page of the book. Ask students to discuss the power of reading an original work versus someone's interpretation or retelling of it: how does that affect the voice of the work? Ask if there is one document they would like to see in person and read firsthand, such as the Constitution of the United States, a handwritten letter from a favorite author, or a letter from a relative who lived several generations ago. Have them write about why reading the original would be more powerful than hearing about it or reading about it in another book or resource. (V, I)

JOURNEY TO THE OTHER SIDE
By Duncan Tonatiuh

One of the most touching moments I have had as an author occurred when a group of fourth graders from Metz Elementary in Austin, Texas, shared with me a multivoice poem they wrote after they read my book *Pancho Rabbit and the Coyote*. This is a link to watch a video of the poem: https://youtu.be/aM6oQEVRyDc.

The students made connections between Pancho's story and their own, and in their poem they shared their families' border-crossing experiences. It was a very rewarding moment, because my book helped the students realize that their stories and their voices are important.

There are an estimated 1.5 million undocumented children in the United States, and according to a 2011 Pew Hispanic Center report, in 2008 there were 5.5 million children of undocumented parents in US schools; the majority of these children are US citizens by birth. Yet of the thousands of children's books that are published in the United States every year, only a handful of them deal with immigrating to this country.

It is important to read and write and celebrate books that reflect a child's experiences and culture. I have noticed that when a young reader sees in a book people who look, talk, or behave like him and his family, that reader feels pride in himself and those around him. I think the fourth graders at Metz Elementary felt that pride when they saw their families' experiences reflected in Pancho's story. The book encouraged them to talk about their journeys, despite the stigma attached to being undocumented or the child of undocumented parents.

Books that deal with immigration are also important for children who are not familiar with border crossing. A book like *Pancho Rabbit* can introduce this topic and spark discussions. Ideally when young readers who are unaware of this issue learn of the harsh journey people—including children like themselves—go through to reach the United States, they'll feel empathy and compassion. Chances are their own classroom contains one of these new-immigrant children.

Our Journeys

A Multivoice Poem
by Ms. Sweet's Fourth Graders, Metz Elementary School, Austin, Texas

> *I'm 10 years old.*
> *I'm in 4th Grade.*
> *I live in the United States.*
>
> *I always have.*
> *I came here when I was a baby.*
> *Yo vine hace 2 años.*
>
> *My parents grew up in the*
> *United States, but my family*
> *speaks Spanish.*
> *My grandpa said they grew up*
> *very poor.*
> *My dad said there was no work*
> >   *in Mexico*
> >   *in Honduras*
> >   *in Guatemala.*
>
> *My mom said we could go to*
> *school in the United States and*
> *have the education she didn't get*
> *to have.*
> *My family decided that we would go.*
>
> *My best friend told me how he*
> *swam across the river.*
> *My mom told me how cold the*
> *water was and how she held me close*
> *because I was just a baby.*
> *My dad said he crossed the desert.*
> *He said he had no food.*

No water.
No shoes.
No money.
That's how my tío died.

My mom tried to come three times
before she got across. I waited for
her for a year.
I came across at night.
We ran.
We were quiet.
We had nothing, just the phone
number of my cousin who would come
pick us up.

Now we are here.
Some of us were born here.
Some of us were carried here
as babies.
Some of us just came here.
Apenas llegué.

But we all want the
same thing.
To learn.
To grow.
To find our way.

I want to be a doctor.
I want to be a vet.
I want to be a teacher.
I want to be an artist.
I want to be an author.

Will you let me? ෨

Chapter 5

THE NITPICKER

WORD CHOICE

The word choice trait is one that teachers and students alike embrace with open arms. Teaching words and how to use them can be satisfying and pleasurable. The goal is to develop a fascination for words. We explore the effect of choosing "just-right" words for the specific purpose and topic; we build confidence with language by growing vocabulary; we encourage accuracy and playfulness with language. We employ figurative language to add deeper meaning and texture to writing. And verbs! We work and work with verbs because they are the power words in sentences. Word choice is the trait that makes all of this happen.

Words are like building blocks. By selecting nouns, verbs, adjectives, adverbs, and every word carefully, writers construct a message. If that message is solid, it sparks the imagination, creates images, and connects—on many levels—with readers. Good word choice brings clarity to the writer's ideas. So word choice, in many ways, is the workhorse trait: it's how writers transform the ordinary into the extraordinary, the mundane into the spectacular. It's how they use language to move, enlighten, and inspire. Word Choice is the nitpicker at the traits dinner party. Others turn to him when the right word or phrase doesn't quite come to mind, and he happily supplies it. He appreciates finer details, and he knows words and how to use them with specificity.

We encourage students to use everyday words when they write informational texts, as well as content-specific words that will explain and engage the reader with the idea. When students write narrative texts, we encourage them to use lively, fresh, and colorful words that have the power to draw in the reader and create a sensory experience. And when students write opinion texts, we encourage them to use compelling and convincing words to elevate the reader to a new level of understanding about their topic. To accomplish all this, writers must develop skills with each of the key qualities of the word choice trait:

- **Using Strong Verbs:** The piece contains many action words, giving it punch and pizzazz. The writer has stretched to find lively verbs that add energy to the piece.
- **Using Striking Words and Phrases:** The piece contains many finely honed words and phrases that make it stand out. The writer employs creative and effective use of alliteration, similes, metaphors, and/or other literary techniques.
- **Using Specific and Accurate Words:** The words are precise, often reflecting content- or information-based vocabulary that the reader needs to understand the message fully. The writer has chosen nouns, adjectives, adverbs, and so forth that create clarity and bring the topic to life.
- **Choosing Words That Deepen Meaning:** The words have been selected to capture the reader's imagination and enhance the piece's meaning. There is a deliberate attempt to choose the best word over the first word that comes to mind.

The Traits Dinner Party: Word Choice

As Word Choice joins the dinner party, it's hard to ignore him. He's a hipster, sporting an expensive, designer flannel shirt, tight-fitting jeans, old-school sneakers, and thick-rimmed glasses. He has a perfectly manicured lumberjack beard, and his nails are obviously trimmed and cared for professionally. His appearance is striking and perfectly suited to the occasion. Word Choice's discriminating taste is apparent as he launches into his spiel about vinyl records, explaining how he prefers the authenticity of the original sound to mainstream digital options. And, as everyone who knows Word Choice can attest, he can talk about the artistic qualities of obscure films at length—and he will, if given any opportunity at all. He's sure of himself and his beliefs, and he uses witty banter to argue passionately and intelligently for alternative points of view.

Word Choice notices the details of the meal and comments not only on the flavor of the dishes but also on the sensory appeal of the entire event. He compliments the table décor, which evokes an appreciative smile from Organization, and he nods in agreement with many of the points Conventions makes. He sits to the left of Voice, whispering in her ear like a conspirator throughout the evening. Word Choice is also an eavesdropper. As others speak, he interjects and then corrects and rephrases what the guest is trying to say more clearly—with annoying frequency. The others forgive him, though, because Word Choice has a knack for chiming in with the right image, the right piece of information, the right question at the ideal time to keep the conversation fresh and lively. His discriminating taste in words and language is deeply admired by all.

Choosing Mentor Texts for the Word Choice Trait

Hint: Don't concern yourself with independent reading level. You want to select books with beautiful language, challenging words, clever turns of phrase, and vivid imagery—sophisticated texts. And that is not a problem, because when you use a picture book or chapter book excerpt as a mentor text, you will be reading aloud to students; students will not be reading them on their own unless that is a choice you both make for other purposes. Fill their heads with models of how words work, even if many of the most outstanding examples are not in their own spoken or written vocabulary—yet. This is how we grow students' knowledge about words and add to their own cache of language choices.

Picture books as mentor texts provide an incredibly rich resource to entice students to write with words and phrases that are specific, accurate, and striking. Contrary to what the average person might think, picture books are far more than simple bedtime stories. Dominic Massaro, a psychology professor at the University of California, Santa Cruz, points out that picture books use engaging language and sophisticated vocabulary: "Reading picture books . . . is stretching them [children] in vocabulary and grammar at an early age. You are preparing them to be expert language users, and indirectly you are going to facilitate their learning to read" (Frey 2015, 2). In other words, reading picture books to students provides the opportunity for growth in word choice and syntax, which are also critical areas for developing writers.

Mine picture books for examples of simple words used with precision, new words invented for the content, dramatic words, content vocabulary words, powerful verbs, words and phrases that conjure visual images or sensory details . . . the list of possibilities goes on and on. As you go on the mentor text word-choice hunt, don't overlook any text—short or long—that has carefully honed language in each of the key qualities:

Using Strong Verbs: Where are the places where the verb really powers the sentence? Where are places where "to be" verbs are used, and why? What is the difference between the active verb and a less energetic one? Do they give the writing energy? Do they make you feel as though the writer wanted to engage you by taking care to use a specific verb with action rather than one that is more ordinary—*zoom* or *bolt* versus *run*, for instance?

Using Striking Words and Phrases: Where are the places in the text that stand out and create a visual image? Is there any evidence of figurative language (similes, metaphors, personification, alliteration, onomatopoeia, and so on)? Does the writing take a risk with words by reaching and stretching via idioms and other wordplay techniques?

Using Specific and Accurate Words: Which words are specific to a content area such as science, math, or social studies, and could expand vocabulary? Has the author chosen words that nail the image—*waterlogged* versus *wet*, for instance? Which parts of speech are used best so that students can appreciate their effect on the clarity of the writing?

Choosing Words That Deepen Meaning: What are the words and phrases that connect the reader to the writer's big idea? Which words were carefully selected and show they were considered carefully over the first word that came to mind? Are there words and phrases that are so creative or imaginative, they lead students to asking questions about the idea and where it might go next?

Word Choice in All Its Glory

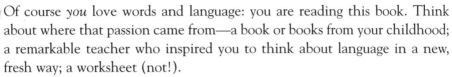

Of course *you* love words and language: you are reading this book. Think about where that passion came from—a book or books from your childhood; a remarkable teacher who inspired you to think about language in a new, fresh way; a worksheet (not!).

One of the hardest things about teaching word choice is knowing when to push and when to ease up. Using everyday words with precision is an excellent goal for students. The words kids know drive their writing, so help them understand that imprecise words and phrases, such as *a place for my stuff*, are less powerful than a more specific choice, such as *backpack* or *locker*. Our students will sprinkle in imagery and high-level vocabulary as they have more exposure to great works that model what students can try next. Be sure to point out specific, powerful word choice in your read-alouds or when you notice these moves in student writing. The nudging we do is delicate and individualized. You don't want to overwhelm or underwhelm when teaching this trait.

Here is a word choice question that comes up frequently: How do we handle text-messaging abbreviations, initialisms, and symbols that show up in student writing? First, we acknowledge that they provide a quick and easy way for students to get words down on paper or screen—the "stuff" of first drafts. They are contemporary and make sense to students in today's world, and yes, I know, they are annoying to teachers. First, we acknowledge that text messaging is not going away. If anything, it's moving faster and faster into mainstream communication.

Use this opportunity to talk about how important it is to consider audience and purpose when we choose our words. Show students just how much it matters that they go back over their first drafts and scrutinize their writing for word choice. Let them determine how differently a piece of writing works when written in text message abbreviations or in standard English. Take a passage from a favorite mentor text and have students translate it into text-messaging abbreviations, initialisms, and emoticons. Then compare the two versions and ask which is likely to inspire the reader more—and why.

Remind students that no one chooses the best words or phrases when drafting. They may think they are the exception, but they aren't. This is a rule that applies to all writers: First drafts are for getting the idea down, not for refining it. It can be in that second or third pass when we revise boring, unclear, and shortcut text-messaging initialisms and abbreviations to make them more precise and in standard language. Just be sure that students understand why it's important that they write in Standard English in their final copies: aside from the issue of readability (conventions), it is also so the writing moves past the simple and obvious and matures using language to convey the message with deeper meaning. This is why students should go the distance to reveal the finesse with language that is ultimately expected of them. And this is why we need mentor texts to show them how it is done.

The goal in teaching this trait should be to develop a fascination with words through reading and writing. Asking questions such as, Why is this word so interesting to us when that one seems more bland? or, How does the alliteration in this passage work to create a sweet-sounding phrase? will get you much, much further than memorizing endless lists of words. Marinate kids in beautiful language, point out what is working and why, and ask for their opinions about the words authors use and how they connect to other traits and the writing as a whole. Inspire curiosity about words and what they mean. Make lists of words that students *want* to try in their pieces. Tantalize them with the possibilities. This is the endgame—the coup de grâce in word choice.

Mentor Texts for the Word Choice Trait: Picture Books

Building on Nature: The Life of Antoni Gaudí
Written by Rachel Rodríguez

Illustrated by Julie Paschkis
Henry Holt, 2009

Antoni Gaudí was a Spanish artist who used nature to inspire his art and architecture. Even when others ridiculed him for his different way of imagining how buildings and shapes could imitate the natural world, Gaudí stayed true to himself. In this biography, readers will be inspired to find their own unique paths through life.

Author Rachel Rodríguez uses precision in her choice of words throughout, such as "Mountain peaks jag against the sky. Silvery olive trees sway in the breeze" (1). Have students go outside and find one natural element to explore by writing about it with descriptive words. Encourage them to focus on color, shape, size, texture, and location to make their descriptions stand out. (WC, I)

Clatter Bash! A Day of the Dead Celebration
Written and Illustrated by Richard Keep
Peachtree, 2004

In a rocking, vibrant, energized picture book, readers explore the Day of the Dead celebration. Sounds, traditions, feelings, and colors fill the pages of this bilingual text, which relies on striking single words, creative hyphenated words, and expressive word combinations to bring the Day of the Dead observances to life.

The text provides an opportunity for readers to see how to express an idea using single words and phrases. Read the text and show the pictures, and then ask students to tell you the big idea of the piece. Challenge them to write and illustrate a new text for a different celebration using single words, hyphenated words, and expressive word phrases modeled in *Clatter Bash!* Take time to note the different use of punctuation marks in Spanish versus English. (WC, C)

Diego Rivera: His World and Ours

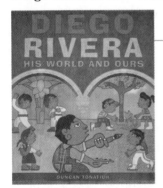

Written and Illustrated by Duncan Tonatiuh
Abrams Books for Young Readers, 2011

Diego Rivera is the subject of several very fine picture books. This version by Tonatiuh is an exquisitely illustrated biography that elucidates Rivera's influences, style, and importance. Written in English, with many embedded words and references that are explained in the detailed glossary and author's note, it's a call to action to create murals and paintings that capture today's rich Latino culture and tell today's stories.

Diego Rivera: His World and Ours sets up the writing for students. Ask kids to think about something of significance that represents Latino culture today—a person, an event, a celebration, and so on—and work together to draw a picture of it or, if possible, a mural. Then ask them to explain the importance of their choice in writing and include it with the art for all to read and enjoy. Encourage them to use specific and interesting words as Tonatiuh modeled in his book on Diego Rivera. (WC, I)

Estas manos: Manitas de mi familia/These Hands: My Family's Hands
Written by Samuel Caraballo
Illustrations by Shawn Costello
Arte Público, 2014

The publisher calls this book an "ode to family," and I have to agree. Caraballo focuses on the hands of each family member and compares them with plants and nature in this loving, gentle tribute. You find out a lot about the character and values of the family as the author uses comparisons and contrasts to enhance each person's best and most memorable attributes.

The technique of comparing a person's qualities with a plant or natural element is one that students could use in their own writing about people who matter to them. Dad's hands are as strong as mahogany trees; Grandma's hands are like magical lilies; brother José's and sister Mariá's hands are like blooming oak trees. Make a list of the different examples from the book and use them to extend the similes and metaphors to help students create an "ode" page or pages of their own. (WC, I)

Frida
Written by Jonah Winter
Illustrated by Ana Juan
Scholastic, 2002

In an inspirational bilingual account of artist Frida Kahlo's life, readers learn that although illness and accidents challenged her every day, art became the means of escaping the pain and loneliness of healing. Frida's art, like her spirit, is admired today because of its passion and how it helps viewers relate to it in a personal way.

Brainstorm words that convey emotion and feeling to describe the book and its subject: *passionate, dedicated, kind, imaginative, painful,* and so on. Look up the corresponding Spanish words with students and write them down. Have the students figure out where to insert some of the words into the flow of the English sentences. For students working with the Spanish text, do the opposite: brainstorm emotion words, look them up in English, and insert them into the sentences in the Spanish text. (WC, V)

Green Is a Chile Pepper: A Book of Colors
Written by Roseanne Greenfield Thong
Illustrated by John Parra
Chronicle Books, 2014

A lighthearted color book full of fun rhyming poems, all of which center on Latino themes, this bilingual book is filled to the brim with vibrant colors and ideas, making it a very readable and enjoyable book for young children.

Assign each student two of the colors from the color palette in the book and then take the class for a walk outside. Ask students to look for examples of their colors in the landscape, buildings, animals, or plants around them. If for some reason they do not see one of their colors, invite them to imagine where the color *might* have been found. Have them draw and write about their observations in a similar style to the book, paying close attention to the descriptive words and phrases in both languages, as was modeled by Thong. (WC, I)

Guacamole: Un poema para cocinar/Guacamole: A Cooking Poem
> **Written by Jorge Argueta**
> Translated by Elisa Amado
> Illustrated by Margarita Sada
> Groundwood Books, 2012

Avocados and guacamole: two of my favorite things. If you've ever wondered how to make the perfect guacamole, this is the book for you! This bilingual procedural text sings off the page with exquisite word choice and lively tempo. You can almost taste every ingredient and feel the energy of making something so yummy. I love this line: "Sing and dance because food tastes better when you sing and dance" (25).

Ask students if they have a favorite food, and work together to write out the steps for making it. Encourage them to get down the basics first, then elaborate with imagination and beautiful language to bring the process to the poetic level. Maybe the recipe could be shared with families and tried out at home! (WC, SF)

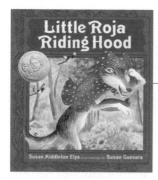

Little Roja Riding Hood
Written by Susan Middleton Elya
Illustrated by Susan Guevara
G. P. Putnam's Sons, 2014

An updated version of a familiar English tale, *Little Roja Riding Hood* draws heavily on Spanish words to spice up the story of the Big Bad Wolf. Young readers will enjoy this *"muy caliente"* take on a familiar fairy tale that's rich with rhyming language and vivid verbs: "While Roja picked blossoms, the wolf sidled off, complete with disguise, to inspect Gram's cough" (8).

Ask students: How does this delightful tale continue? What becomes of the wolf? Does he learn a lesson? Have students work in groups to fashion a sequel for this traditional fairy tale using Spanish and English words that rhyme and active verbs that enliven it. (And they can punctuate dialogue correctly for conventions practice.) (WC, C)

My Abuelita
Written by Tony Johnston
Illustrated by Yuyi Morales
HMH Books for Young Readers, 2009
Pura Belpré Illustrator Honor Award

A grandson's loving description of his *abuelita* lies at the heart of this book. He knows he has the most amazing grandmother of all time, and each page is filled with descriptions of what makes her remarkable—and the grandmother we all want, too. Told in English with a few Spanish words, the story has a secret, and clues are hidden along the way: What is Abuelita's job? For what is she preparing? The book offers example after example of exquisitely written language.

"She always says words should be as round as dimes and as wild as blossoms blooming," relates Abuelita's grandson (16). Ask students to pick a phrase from this text and explain why it stands out to them, as well as what they see in their minds when they hear it or read it. As they dig deeply into their choices, ask students to notice elements of figurative language or how Tony Johnston used words in new ways to make the writing stand out. (WC, I)

The Old Man and His Door/El viejo y su puerta
Written by Gary Soto
Illustrated by Joe Cepeda
G. P. Putnam's Sons, 1996

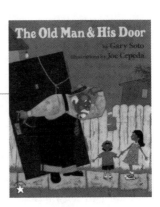

The old man's wife asks for a *puerco* (pig), but he hears it differently: *puerta* (door). And so begins this delightful tale of how the old man finds a *puerta* and the adventures that happens as he brings it home to his surprised wife. A useful glossary of Spanish terms is provided, and a Spanish edition is also available.

Have students find two words that are similar or rhyme in English and/or Spanish: *gato* (cat) and *pato* (duck), or *capa* (cape) and *mapa* (map), for example. Ask students to write a play that shows what high jinks take place if the main character mixes up the two words. (WC, I)

Side by Side/Lado a lado: The Story of Dolores Huerta and Cesar Chavez/ La historia de Dolores Huerta y César Chávez

Written by Monica Brown
Illustrated by Joe Cepeda
Rayo, 2010

In a magnificent tribute to two of the most influential political and human rights activists of the twentieth century, Delores Huerta and Cesar Chavez, this bilingual picture book celebrates the journey of migrant farmworkers to gain rights and improve working conditions in the United States. Out of this movement came many changes and a phrase that resonates today as much as ever: "¡Sí, se puede! Yes, we can!"

Ask students to read and discuss the importance of Huerta and Chavez's legacy. Use the notes in the back of the book for further background and details to share with students. Then ask students to consider the phrase "¡Sí, se puede! Yes, we can!" and how it might apply to something that is going on in their life that they feel is unfair and needs to be changed for the benefit of all. Have them write a short opinion piece about their cause and be sure to use the "¡Sí, se puede! Yes, we can!" phrase to anchor their opinion. (WC, I)

Siesta
Written by Ginger Foglesong Guy
Illustrated by René King Moreno
HarperCollins, 2005
ALA Notable Children's Book, Younger Readers Award

With this simple and sweet story about a brother and sister preparing to take an afternoon nap, readers will want to climb right into the blanket tent and enjoy the experience, too. English and Spanish names for colors and objects pepper the vibrant pages. This book is warm and rich— and definitely one readers of all ages will want to return to over and over.

Try making a chart for students to fill in the English and Spanish vocabulary words throughout the book that so perfectly describe everyday objects. Then ask students to list the favorite things they'd bring to a tent to prepare for a summer's siesta. Finally, take a close look at the different types of sentences in *Siesta* and the use of questions to make the piece flow smoothly throughout, and challenge students to write a short piece that uses both statements and questions as they describe their perfect napping place. (WC, SF)

What Can You Do with a Paleta?/¿Qué puedes hacer con una paleta?
Written by Carmen Tafolla
Illustrated by Magaly Morales
Dragonfly Books, 2009

A *paleta*, a delicious, frozen ice cream treat, is just the thing for a hot summer's day. This bilingual story uses vivid description to explain what a paleta is and how wonderful it can be to cool you off when you need it most. The book is a fine example of informational text with style!

Tell students to think about what their own hot weather treat might be and describe it so clearly that someone could tell what it is, what it looks like, how it tastes, how it feels going down the throat, and all the places it might be found. Encourage them to be creative in their descriptions of their delicious goody. (WC, I)

The Woman Who Outshone the Sun/La mujer qui brillaba aún mas que el sol
From a poem by Alejandro Cruz Martinez
Story by Rosalma Zubizarreta, Harriet Rohmer, and David Schecter
Illustrated by Fernando Olivera
Lee and Low Books, 1991
American Library Association Notable Book

When Lucia Zenteno arrives in town, she dazzles everyone with her beauty and light. They have no idea where she came from, but they're amazed by her powers. The old people of the village think she should be honored and respected, but the young people are afraid of Lucia Zenteno and are very rude to her. Lucia leaves, and takes the river—the source of life—with her, causing everyone to try to find her and beg her forgiveness. Kindness and compassion rule the day, and the villagers learn a valuable lesson.

Ask students to brainstorm synonyms for *kindness* and write them in both English and Spanish. List other words that might describe a person's character, as well—*honesty, integrity, loyalty,* and so on—and create illustrated posters of the words in both languages. (WC, V)

Mentor Texts for the Word Choice Trait: Chapter Books

90 Miles to Havana
Written by Enrique Flores-Galbis
Roaring Brook, 2010
Pura Belpré Honor Book for Narrative, 2011 Bank Street Best Children's Book of the Year, A Sunshine State Young Reader's Award Selection

To really show what a revolution is, you have to draw at least three pictures. A before, a during, and then an after . . . Bebo picks up five brown eggs in his big hand. "This is before," he says, holding up the eggs like a magician about to make them disappear. "Inside these eggs are all the important things that everybody needs: schools, houses, food, and money. For one reason or another a few people have gotten hold of all the eggs and they don't want to share them." Then he starts cracking one egg after the other. The slippery yokes slide out and chase one another around the white bowl. "This is during. Things get smashed and crack, everything gets cut loose, and everybody starts grabbing. That's what we saw last night. It's what's happening now," he says as he pokes at the five yokes with a fork and then scrambles them into one big yellow lake. (22–23)

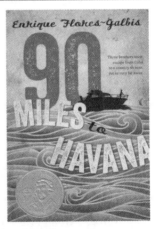

Based on a true story from Operation Pedro Pan 1961, during which 14,000 refugee children were evacuated to the United States during the Cuban Revolution, this book is a jam-packed adventure story from beginning to end. The story touches on every possible emotion as you find yourself rooting for Julian and his brothers to defy the odds and make it to safety.

Ask students to discuss the metaphorical definition of *revolution* and their understanding of the word from Bebo's explanation that uses eggs. Then look up the dictionary definition of *revolution* and compare it with Bebo's. Discuss how figurative language helps readers understand complex ideas, such as how citizens of a country are affected before, during, and after a revolution. To reveal the rest of the metaphor, read aloud the paragraph that follows the exemplar passage in the book.

Have students write opinion pieces about whether the dictionary definition of *revolution* or Bebo's metaphor was more effective communicating the big idea, supporting their opinions with clear rationale. Ask those who feel ready to apply a new metaphor to another event with a before, during, and after phase, using figurative language to create imagery that reveals the full effect of that event to the reader. Consider topics that require research, too, such as the invention of the atom bomb, the creation of a vaccine for HIV, the movement to establish the District of Columbia as a state, the science of global warming, the effect of big-game hunting, and so on. Students should focus on complex topics with far-reaching effects. (WC, I)

Becoming Naomi León/Yo, Naomi León
Written by Pam Muñoz Ryan
Scholastic, 2004

Chewing on the end of my pencil, I got back to my list, which Gram said was one of the things I did best. I had all kinds of lists in my notebook, the shortest being "Things I Am Good At" which consisted of 1) Soap carving, 2) Worrying, and 3) Making lists.

There was my "Regular and Everyday Worries" list, which included 1) Gram was going to die because she was old, 2) Owen would never be right, 3) I will forget something if I don't make a list, 4) I will lose my lists, and 5) Abominations. I made lists of splendid words, types of rocks, books I read, and unusual names. Not to mention the lists I had copied, including "Baby Animal Names," "Breeds of Horses," and my current favorite, "Animal Groups from The Complete and Unabridged Animal Kingdom with over 200 Photographs." (9)

Naomi Soledad León Outlaw has a complicated life. She has a unique last name, her clothes don't look like the other kids', she's painfully shy and has trouble speaking up, and no one at school seems to notice her at all. Naomi lives with her gram and her little brother in a tidy little trailer where all goes fairly well until her mother shows up, which causes chaos in young Naomi's life. One of the ways Naomi learns to cope is through her love of words and reading. Naomi creates a "Splendid Words" list in English. Then, as she comes to understand more about her father and her heritage, she decides to keep a "Splendid Words" list in Spanish.

Ask students to think about words that intrigue them. Maybe they will notice the word *abominations* from the passage and wonder what is meant—which might inspire further reading and talking. Post a "Splendid Words" list in English and one in Spanish, and ask students to add the words they like while keeping an eye open for new words to add as they read and write going forward. "Splendid Words" lists in other languages can be added as well. (WC, V)

The Color of My Words/El color de mis palabras
Written by Lynn Joseph
HarperCollins, 2001
The Americas Award for Children's and Young Adult Literature

"Words"
May I have some paper, please
Please, may I have some paper
'Cause these words of mine
go walk away
they go walk away all by themselves
and get lost in the crowd.

May I have some paper, please
Please may I have some paper
To catch these words
and wrap them up
where they can't walk away
slip off the edge
and drown. (10)

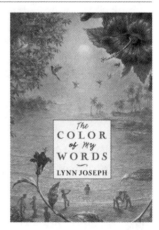

Kirkus Reviews gave this text a starred review: "An achingly beautiful story." Each chapter of *The Color of My Words* begins with a poem followed by the account behind it, all adding up to a complete, astonishing story that will break your heart. Twelve-year-old Ana Rosa lives in a country where words are seen as powerful political weapons—and where writing is discouraged. Ana Rosa struggles to find her voice, to transform the world and all of its tragedies through her powerful writing.

This chapter provides an excellent opportunity for students to begin using writer's notebooks so they can capture the words and images that matter to them for use in future writing. Writer's notebooks can be created or purchased, whichever works best. Begin by having students capture a list of their ten favorite words so they "can't walk away, slip off the edge, and drown." Then brainstorm together different types of lists to keep so students continue to think about and collect words. (WC, I)

The Dreamer/El soñador
Written by Pam Muñoz Ryan
Translated by Iñigo Javaloyes
Illustrated by Peter Sís
Scholastic, 2010
Pura Belpré Award, Boston Globe-Honor Book Award, ALA Notable

Neftalí? To which mystical land does an unfinished staircase lead? (16)

What grows in the dark soil of disappointment? (132)

In the largest of worlds, what adventures await the smallest of ships? (150)

Who spins the elaborate web that entraps the timid spirit? (266)

When Neftalí wrote thoughts or poems, he felt whole. Writing poetry was his passion, his gift. Yet his father did not support his poetic calling. Although Neftalí tried to open his father's mind, ultimately he had to part from his family to become his true self. Daydreaming and imagining stories and ideas led to writings of political protest in support of nature and the rights of indigenous Chilean people. *The Dreamer* is a fictionalized biography of Pablo Neruda and a sensational, lyrical account of the famous poet's life and accomplishments. As author Pam Muñoz Ryan explains, "I hope readers will retreat into their own wandering thoughts and imagine answers." Refer to the endnotes for historical background on the remarkable life of Pablo Neruda.

This magnificent book is a treasure trove of beautiful language. The questions that are spotlighted throughout the text can serve as great jumping-off points for writing, too. Ask students to choose one they relate to and write their ideas freely—in prose or poetry—expressing their deepest thoughts, using words that enhance the meaning as Neftalí did. (WC, SF)

Esperanza Rising/Esperanza renace
Written by Pam Muñoz Ryan
Scholastic, 2000
Pura Belpré Award, Jane Addams Children's Book Award Winner, ALA Top
Ten Best Books for Young Adults

> *She [Esperanza] had her family, a garden full of roses, her faith, and the memories of those who had gone before her. But now, she had even more than that, and it carried her up, as on the wings of the phoenix. She soared with the anticipation of dreams she never knew she could have, of learning English, of supporting her family, of someday buying a tiny house. Miguel had been right about never giving up, and she had been right, too, about rising above those who held them down.* (249–50)

Esperanza leads a fairy-tale life compared with many other people. The Mexican Revolution, however, changes that life drastically. Bandits capture and kill her father. Her awful stepbrother takes over her father's estate, and Esperanza and her mother flee to California, where a life of hard labor and financial struggles challenges her to find a way to be happy despite her circumstances. This is a beautifully fluent text, a trademark of author Pam Muñoz Ryan, with lyrical sentence structure and careful attention to the sound and choice of the words throughout.

Read the passage, or any other passage you select from *Esperanza Rising*, to students. Ask them to close their eyes and hear the rhythm of the words and imagine the scene or feelings in their minds. Then ask them to draw a picture and write a caption about what the words mean to them. Or, ask them to write a poem that captures the feeling in the passage. (WC, SF)

Lowriders in Space (Book 1)
Written by Cathy Camper
Illustrated by Raul the Third
Chronicle Books, 2014

> *Elirio Malaria, Flapjack Octopus, and Lupe Impala liked working with cars. That was their job.*
>
> *Lupe Impala was the finest mechanic south of Vacaville. She could rescue a dropped gasket, notch a belt, or electrocharge a spark plug, swish a swashplate, or wrangle a manifold with a twist of her wrench and a flick of her wrist. Lupe Impala: Mechanic Extraordinaire.* (8–9)

Flapjack Octopus wielded the wettest washcloth north of the Salton Sea. When he polished a car, he spun over the paint job like an eight-pointed ninja star flying through the night. All the cars on the lot gleamed from his expertise. (11)

Elirio was the best detail artist around. People were a little afraid of Elirio Malaria. With a beak like that, they thought he might bite.
[Bubble by Elirio:] Don't be scared, eses! Only lady mosquitos bite vatos for food. (13)

Where to begin describing this absolutely amazing graphic novel? First, let's start with the topic: three characters who simply *love* working with cars, especially low riders that "hip, hop, dip, and drop." There's a contest for the best car, so the team opens a shop and tries to turn the junker they have into the best car in the universe. Oh, and did I mention *universe* is not hyperbole? This is literally an out-of-this-world story.

Readers will appreciate the graphic novel style, the Spanish words and phrases that are footnoted and in a glossary at the back, and the fresh voices in narration and dialogue. And how I wish we could show you the drawings here!

Students will want to read this book and read it *now*. To turn their excitement about this imaginative and highly engaging book into a mentor text for writing, share the character descriptions and ask students if the use of similes helped them picture each one. And ask why, in their opinion, author Cathy Camper chose not to use figurative language when describing Elirio Malaria. If possible, show students the illustrations from the book to see how the words and their mental images match up.

Challenge students to add a fourth character to the basics of what they know about the story and to write his or her description in the same style as that of Lupe Impala and Flapjack Octopus. Encourage them to have fun with the names and use words creatively to introduce them to readers. Have them add art if possible. (I can't wait for Book 2 and any others in this series!) (WC, V)

TOWARD WHOLENESS AND BEAUTY: A WRITER'S PERSPECTIVE
by Monica Brown

I am the daughter of a North American father and a South American mother. When I was young, my mother told me that I was a citizen of the world, and I believed it. I have been inspired to write by my own experiences—my life and that of my siblings, my cousins, and my own children. I grew up with a fluid idea of borders—traveling between the United States and Peru, and in a family that was Catholic and Jewish. The people I loved were spread over several continents, and I was a child of the Américas. When my daughters were born, however, I looked around and found very few picture books that reflected the multiplicity and richness of our experiences as biracial, bicultural children. Today, I write for the children of the Américas, as well as children across the globe. My work has been translated into seven languages, and I delight in this wonder of words and art connecting people and cultures.

My mother, Isabel Maria Vexler Valdivieso, was born in Piura, Peru, and she was one of my greatest inspirations. She was an amazing artist who nurtured me and inspired me. I grew up surrounded by her paintings, which I realize helped me think visually and write better for the artists I collaborate with. Picture books are, after all, the meeting place of text and art. In the present, the way I nurture my own creativity is to be open to the magic and wildness and challenges of living each and every day. Laughter is a big part of that; searching out new experiences is part of that; and being engaged in my community, large and small. I read a lot and surround myself with art—my mother's, local artists', and art by folks such as John Parra and Rafael Lopez, my collaborators.

I love creating books that are bilingual, with my two beautiful languages, English and Spanish, side by side on the page. I believe children's books can enhance and even transform the modern classroom and curriculum. To me, their ability to do that is as important as any textbook ever written. The very best of literature, with its beautiful, inspiring, and powerful texts, can electrify students and engage them in ways that exercises and test preparation cannot. And, at the same time, reading children's books still supports important skills such as critical thinking and interpreting.

With my picture book biographies of figures such as Gabriel García Márquez (*My Name Is Gabito: The Life of Gabriel García Márquez/Me llamo Gabito: La vida de Gabriel García Márquez*), Dolores Huerta and Cesar Chavez (*Side by Side/Lado a lado: The Story of Dolores Huerta and Cesar Chavez/La historia de Dolores Huerta y César Chávez*), and Pablo Neruda (*Pablo Neruda: Poet of the People*), I celebrate the lives of extraordinary Latino/as and share the rich contributions Latino/as have made to the Américas and beyond.

I've also gotten a great deal of pleasure from creating characters such as Marisol McDonald (*Marisol McDonald Doesn't Match/Marisol McDonald no combina*) and Lola Levine (*Lola Levine Is Not Mean!*), children who are unique and funny, creative and nonconformist. Their stories explore what it means to be a little different, to see the world a little differently, to maybe experience teasing because of that difference. My characters find the resolution, humor, and family support to move forward with fierceness and love. These characters are the present and the inevitable future—one that crosses borders and boundaries.

We need to raise our children to be proud of their multiethnic heritage and to explore the multiplicity of their own being. We need to think beyond boxes and labels, because so many of us never fit in just one in the first place! Perhaps it is the border-dwellers—those of us who straddle multiple cultures and communities—who can help us celebrate our connectedness. I hope the literature I create inspires children to open their minds and hearts to the wholeness and beauty within us all. ◉

Chapter 6

THE CONVERSATIONALIST

SENTENCE FLUENCY

Welcome to the sentence fluency roller-coaster ride. At first the action feels controlled, and you wonder what all the fuss is about. It doesn't feel scary at all. You gradually pick up speed by learning different sentence types and how they are constructed. But as the ride continues, it moves faster and faster, through loops and turns of sentences that are correct, measured, different in style and length, but also fluent—they pull you high above the ground, then drop you so fast your stomach lurches. The wild wind blows your hair straight out. The skin on your face presses flat against your skull. You can't help but smile and whoop: the exhilaration! The jolt! The frisson! These sentences are intent on thrilling their readers, and they are not for the faint of heart. They are also the sentences that make writing so much more magnificent than any kiddie ride at the writing fair.

Sentence fluency is about how words and phrases flow through a piece of writing. It is achieved when the writer pays close attention to the way individual sentences are crafted and groups of sentences are combined.

One way writers create fluency is by employing different types of sentences within a single piece. They might use compound sentences to add detail, immerse the reader in information, and reinforce a point. They might use short, declarative sentences to drive that point home. And fragments?

Writers might use sentence fragments to isolate an important thought and make the reader stand up and take notice of it. Sentence fluency adds pacing and rhythm to writing. Just as a musician crafts a beautiful song, a writer crafts a fluent piece of writing by varying sentence structures and lengths, and paying very close attention to how those sentences sound when they're brought together.

Writing fluently is not simple, because it requires the writer to conjure up everything he or she knows about language—how it works, how it looks, how it sounds, how it touches the person receiving it—to find the best approach for the piece. In other words, a fluent writer must apply the following key qualities with skill and confidence:

- **Crafting Well-Built Sentences:** The sentences are carefully and creatively constructed for maximum effect. Transition words such as *but, and*, and *so* are used successfully to join sentences and sentence parts.
- **Varying Sentence Types:** A variety of sentence types (simple, compound, and/or complex) enhance the central theme or story line. The piece is made up of an effective mix of long, complex sentences and short, simple ones.
- **Capturing Smooth and Rhythmic Flow:** The writer has thought about how the sentences sound. If the piece were to be shared aloud, it would be easy on the ear. The writer uses phrasing that sounds almost musical and is therefore a joy to read.
- **Breaking the Rules to Create Fluency:** The sentences diverge from Standard English to create interest and effect when appropriate. For example, there may be sentence fragments, such as *all alone in the forest*, or a single word, such as *Bam!*, to accent a particular moment or action. Sentences might begin with informal words such as *well, and*, or *but* to create a conversational tone, or rules may be broken intentionally to make dialogue sound authentic.

The Traits Dinner Party: Sentence Fluency

Because Sentence Fluency is a Gemini on the astrological chart, she looks at things from two points of view: definitive *and* flexible. Her training in classical ballet centered on form as well as rhythm, so she's deeply steeped in the function of both. She arrives at our party adorned in a flowing gown and artfully tied African headscarf; the stunning blue and white lace appears to flow like a river as she glides gracefully into the room. The other trait guests are captivated by her posture, her bearing, her elegant strides. The soft hand-beaded leather sandals on her feet barely whisper with each step.

When Sentence Fluency finally settles down at the table, she sits next to longtime colleague Conventions, who has come to appreciate her dramatic nature but also appreciates her sense of certainty. She kisses Conventions elegantly on both cheeks, noting that without his influence over the years, her style and her unique sense of rhythm and flow could never have developed so completely. Sentence Fluency is talkative, versatile, and eloquent, and she mingles cleverly with her fellow traits. She engages them in long discussions punctuated by short, enthusiastic outbursts. "Yes!" she cries out when Word Choice makes a clever point. Ideas watches Sentence Fluency work the room, noting her gift for gab and command of language—her Gemini tendencies in full glory. Toward the end of the evening, Sentence Fluency performs a dance she choreographed just for this occasion while Conventions accompanies her on the piano, grumbling about how some of her impromptu moves force him to deviate from the score. The other guests have come to anticipate this unique entertainment from their friend at gatherings like this, and they are completely entranced by her grace and expressiveness.

Choosing Mentor Texts for the Sentence Fluency Trait

Finding fluent sentences in mentor texts means doing something most of us love: reading aloud. This is one of my favorite things to do with students—and for myself. I read a book over and over, trying to capture the rhythm and cadence the author intended before I share it with students. As I'm reading, I'm listening for the sound of the words and phrases. And when I find those that sing off the page, I mark them so I know to point them out on a second, third, or fourth reading with the students. You'll hear beautiful fluency in some of the picture books you find, even those with a sparse number of words. Many are poetic—they are just that lyrical. Here are some questions to ask yourself as you consider a book as a mentor text for the sentence fluency trait:

Crafting Well-Built Sentences: Are there different types of sentences that are grammatically well constructed? Has the author used coordinating conjunctions such as *but, and,* and *so* to connect parts of sentences?

How are clauses and phrases used in the sentences to expand them and still be grammatically correct?

Varying Sentence Types: Can you find examples of simple, compound, and/or complex sentences? How many simple sentences are there compared with compound and/or complex sentences? Have sentence types been repeated for an effect? Do the sentences all begin in the same way, or is there variety?

Capturing Smooth and Rhythmic Flow: Is it easy to read this piece aloud? Where is the phrasing particularly smooth? What literary devices has the writer used to create fluency and smooth-flowing text? Alliteration? Amplification? Euphony? Parallelism? Stream of consciousness?

Breaking the Rules to Create Fluency: Has the author taken risks with sentences? Are there fragments? Are there single words that stand alone? Has the author tried to use punctuation such as dashes, ellipses, or semicolons to make the sentences flow smoothly? Do the sentences begin informally to be authentic to the scene—a conversational tone, for instance, to indicate dialogue between friends?

Thoughts About Sentence Fluency: The Sound and the Fury

Sentence fluency is not a silent trait—it's actually quite a noisy one. Writers must read their writing aloud to hear the rhythm of the phrases and sentences. It's the only way for them to hear how well the sentences work and where they still need attention. When you hear language aloud, a lot, you develop a regulator in your ear that whispers, "Hmm . . . that's not quite right. What about moving this word here and that phrase to the beginning of the sentence? Now, yes . . . that sounds better." We can develop a sense for where sentences start and stop and which words and phrases are humming along and which are clunky. That is why I call sentence fluency the auditory trait. We "read" for it with the ear as much as the eye. And that's what makes it noisy.

Imagine being a student who is new to English because your first language—the one you've heard as a small child, the language you came to know like breathing—is not what is being spoken around you or represented in books you are trying to read. Many of our students speak home languages that sound remarkably different from English, yet English permeates the air. They hear English on TV, in music, on the radio, and, of course, in school. But when they try to replicate what they hear, it doesn't sound smooth right away. It will take a long time and many, many years to gain the confidence to write as smoothly in English as sentence fluency requires. This is another way, though, that the mentor texts noted in this book can help: When we read aloud as often as possible from these books, especially those that are bilingual or contain Spanish words, students gain exposure to English in a way that becomes familiar and comfortable. They hear how the words sound, they can practice with pattern and rhythm, *and* they hear their own language and see the culture represented in the book, which reminds them how valuable it is to have access to both.

The majority of student writers I've met over the years are challenged by the sentence fluency trait, no matter what their language of origin. All students need our patience, coupled with thousands of read-alouds so they can hear the phrasing of the English language, to soar in sentence fluency. All students. But again, imagine how high each literacy hurdle looms for a child who is just beginning to speak English: first understanding English words, then trying to speak them, and eventually reading and writing in English. Children do learn and master English sentences, however, because they are driven to succeed, because their teachers care, and because their options in life depend on it.

My friend David L. Harrison, a poet and children's author, wrote a poem that describes beautifully the importance of sentence fluency—as well as the importance of *hearing* our sentences read aloud:

The Sound of a Sentence

A sentence can poke turtle-like on a page.
It can leap like an antelope playing.
It can vary from short to the lengthier sort,
Depending on what you are saying.

When you read with your eye and hear with your ear,
Your readers will love what you're writing.
A balance of turtle and antelope sentences
Helps make your piece exciting.

"He screamed!" is a sentence both short and direct.
It grabs us. It holds our attention.

But where *he screamed and* why *he screamed*
Deserve more than two words to mention.

So vary the patterns and go with the flow
And polish the lines 'til they glisten.
Learn if you've done what you set out to do,
Read it aloud, and listen.

Mentor Texts for the Sentence Fluency Trait: Picture Books

Action Jackson
Written by Jan Greenberg and Sandra Jordan
Illustrated by Robert Andrew Parker
Macmillan, 2007
A Sibert Honor Book, New York Times Best
Book of the Year, Publishers Weekly Best Book
of the Year

A beautiful and eloquent description of what might have been an ordinary day of extraordinary thoughts in the life of the artist Jackson Pollock. Readers explore how a talented artist took inspiration for his art from Mexican traditions as he pursued his dream to find his own style and voice as a painter.

This text has an elegant flow: "Hours go by like minutes" and "An insect lands in the wet paint, and there it stays." The flow of the sentences builds strong images for the reader. Ask students to find a favorite passage in the text and note other phrases that add to the fluency of the writing. (SF, V)

The Cazuela That the Farm Maiden Stirred
Written by Samantha R. Vamos
Illustrated by Rafael López
Charlesbridge, 2013
Pura Belpré Illustrator Honor Award, ALA Notable
Children's Book

"This is the pot that the farm maiden stirred" is the opening line to this cumulative tale reminiscent of the Mother Goose rhyme "The House That Jack Built." This story, however, is told in English with the clever use of Spanish words and phrases on the next page to build the story bilingually. The story is about making rice pudding, and the recipe is provided at the end, along with a detailed glossary of Spanish words. The rhythm, the words, the glorious art—this book is a winner for sure.

Repeating patterns that build page to page can be a fun way for students to try writing a piece similar to *The Cazuela That the Farm Maiden Stirred* on their own or as a class. Have students select a food and think about all the steps that go into creating it. They can write the cumulative story and provide a recipe, just as Samantha Vamos models in the text. (SF, WC, O)

Drum Dream Girl: How One Girl's Courage Changed Music

Written by Margarita Engle
Illustrated by Rafael López
HMH Books for Young Readers, 2015
2015 Pura Belpré Illustrator Award

Inspiration, wordsmithery, and elegant prose fill the pages of this book about the drum dream girl. No one believes a girl can or should play the drums, so the drum dream girl practices in secret with her own imaginary music, which is based on the world around her. Eventually, her talent is discovered and she joins a newly formed all-girl band—which her traditional-minded father comes to support.

This lyrical prose reads aloud beautifully. Share it with students and then stop and point out the varied techniques that Engle uses to make the piece so fluent: alliteration, repetition, long sentences that flow from page to page, and exquisite word choice. Ask students to choose a page that stands out and write about the ways the author used sentence fluency to make the book strong—and challenge them to use those same techniques in their opinions and explanations. (SF, WC)

Funny Bones: Posada and His Day of the Dead Calaveras

Written and Illustrated by Duncan Tonatiuh
Abrams, 2015
2015 Robert F. Sibert Informational Book Award,
2015 Pura Belpré Illustrator Honor Award

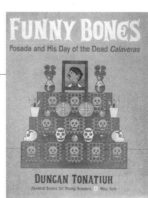

Read about the life and art of Guadalupe (Lupe) Posada (1852–1913) in this page-turning biography. *Funny Bones* explains how *calaveras* (funny, decorative skeletons) originated and the process by which Posada created and refined his art over the years. Richly textured illustrations lead the reader through page after page of fascinating and well-researched information.

Look at the way Tonatiuh has used different sentence types to create focus and purpose throughout the text. He uses a variety of well-crafted sentences to tell Posada's life story, adds step-by-step directions that are short and show parallel structure, and inserts questions about different topics throughout the book. Invite students to justify and write their opinions about any of the questions posed in the book on *calaveras* or other topics on the question pages, and have them share in small groups what they think and why based on evidence from the text or new research they may conduct. (SF, O)

Gracias/Thanks
Written by Pat Mora
Spanish translation by Adriana Domínguez
Illustrated by John Parra
Lee and Low Books, 2009
Pura Belpré Honor Book

What are you thankful for? Be they small or large, there are many special moments in life to note and show gratitude for. *Gracias/Thanks* covers each idea with a light heart, charming personal insights, and heartfelt appreciation. Written in phrases that begin "For . . ." that develop the notion of gratitude, we find out the young boy in the book is thankful for many wonderful things in his everyday life: the sun, his *abuelita*, fishing worms, foamy waves, and more.

Have students write their own Gracias/Thanks book of multiple things they are grateful for. Show them the phrasing pattern from the book, and have them create their own list with explanations modeled from the mentor text. Bind all their ideas together and create a classroom book, *Gracias/Thanks from [your classroom]*, and leave it out for all to enjoy and read aloud to each other. (SF, I)

Mango, Abuela, and Me
Written by Meg Medina
Illustrated by Angela Dominguez
Candlewick, 2015
2015 Pura Belpré Honor Book, 2015 Pura Belpré
Illustrator Honor Award

Language and its value is the focus of this tender story. When Mia's "far-away" grandmother comes to live with Mia and her family, she doesn't know English well enough to share bedtime stories with Mia. A natural-born teacher, Mia uses common interests to add words to Abuela's vocabulary, but things really take a turn for the better when a parrot joins the household and becomes the best teacher of all.

The book is a model text for sentences of all types—long and short, and with many different constructions. Dialogue, something that students have trouble handling well, punctuates the piece throughout. Ask students to read and enjoy the book with you, and then challenge them to create dialogue between the parrot and a learner of English, using words and phrases the parrot could repeat. Have students pay special attention to the different sentence constructions that emphasize the words that matter most in their conversations. (SF, WC)

Martina the Beautiful Cockroach: A Cuban Folktale

Retold by Carmen Agra Deedy
Illustrated by Michael Austin
Peachtree, 2007

Martina's beloved *abuela* offers her a secret test to find the perfect husband. Doubtful but willing, Martina tries it out, and one by one, her suitors fail! Until . . . a special matched suitor finds her heart (and foot). This beautifully illustrated and charming story is written in English with a few Spanish words scattered in. It is also available in an award-winning Spanish and English audio version, read by the author, who is a world-class storyteller.

Ask students to create another suitor to add to this story and figure out how Abuela's test will work for that person. Have them write it in dialogue, as modeled in the book, and help them figure out where they would add the suitor into the existing text. Show the different ways Deedy creates fluent dialogue: (1) breaking up what is said aloud with the name of the speaker in the middle of a sentence, (2) adding who is speaking at the end of the sentence, and (3) leaving out the name of the speaker in the sentence. Point out the conventions of using dialogue: punctuation and indenting. (SF, C)

Maya's Blanket/La manta de Maya

Written by Monica Brown
Illustrated by David Diaz
Children's Book Press, 2015

Maya has a special *manta* (blanket) she loves. But as it is used, it becomes worn and frayed and much smaller, so her *abuelita* makes it into a vest. The vest becomes a *falda* (skirt) as the amount of usable fabric becomes smaller and smaller over time. Based on a Yiddish folk song, this story has a cumulative sentence fluency element—tying together the first use of the fabric in each new iteration.

Students will enjoy hearing the repetition and even joining in as you read. Ask them what Maya's daughter's magical manta at the end of the book might become as she loves it over time. Have them write out a series of sentences that work together smoothly, showing how it goes from the manta to other creative uses of the fabric until it is but a small remnant of the original. (SF, WC)

Mice and Beans/Arroz con frijoles
Written by Pam Muñoz Ryan
Illustrated by Joe Cepeda
Scholastic, 2001

Rosa Maria is getting her house ready for a fabulous birthday celebration, each day prepping something new. And each day, mischievous little mice help themselves to bits of what Rosa Maria has prepared. She sets traps for the mice each night, only to discover that the mice have, in fact, prepared something she forgot. After a series of events that each end with "She hurried to the cupboard to fetch another and when it was set and ready to snap, she turned off the light and went to bed," Rosa Maria learns that even a mouse deserves to be in her house!

Come up with a repeating refrain such as "They cleaned up the terrible mess and emptied the trash one more time, and then they took their backpacks and headed home for the night." Ask students to think of a story with a bit of a mystery that could develop, using this anchor line on every page. (SF, I)

My Granny Went to Market/Abuelita fue al mercado
Written by Stella Blackstone
Illustrated by Christopher Corr
Barefoot Books, 1995

In this rhyming, counting picture book, readers travel around the world, stopping in different locations to get a quick feel for the place and its customs. The text is available in Spanish and English, and although only two of the stops are countries with Latino heritage, Mexico and Peru, it is a book about world cultures that all students will enjoy.

One of the things that readers discover on every page is a cultural image from each country: a paper lantern from China, a nesting doll from Russia, llamas and a magic carpet from Peru, and so on. Ask groups of students to pick ten items that reflect American culture and write their own counting, rhyming books using *My Granny Went to Market* as a model. (SF, O)

My Name Is Celia: The Life of Celia Cruz/ Me llamo Celia: La vida de Celia Cruz
Written by Monica Brown
Illustrated by Rafael López
Luna Rising, 2004
America's Book Award

Cuban-born salsa queen Celia Cruz led an inspiring life. Rich with imagery and lively descriptions, the bilingual book is a tribute to this musical and talented woman. Its rhythm and tempo make you want to dance as you read it aloud.

Ask students to focus on the introduction to the book and how author Monica Brown engages readers and draws us into the text. Note the different sensory images that are used in the introduction, and invite students to write an introduction to their autobiography that uses many of the same techniques as Brown. (SF, O)

Round Is a Tortilla
Written by Roseanne Greenfield Thong
Illustrated by John Parra
Chronicle Books, 2015
Texas 2x2 Reading List Selection, A Bank Street College of Education Best Book of the Year, ALA Notable Children's Book nominee

Simple, delightful, and certain to help writers think differently, this book compares shapes with everyday objects: triangles are crunchy chips; square is the park and the *zócalo* (main town square); round are *comanas* that chime and ring; and so on. Readers are invited to find shapes in our everyday environment. The glossary in the back helps non-Spanish-speakers learn some of the Spanish words sprinkled throughout the text.

Take students on a walk outside with paper and pencils. Have them draw the shapes they see in the schoolyard, on the street, all around them. Using the format from the book as a model, ask students to create a rhythmic piece about one or two of the shapes they discovered, and put all their examples together in one class book. Encourage the class to choose a title using *Round Is a Tortilla* as inspiration. (SF, WC)

The Runaway Piggy/El cochinito fugitivo
Written by James Luna
Illustrated by Laura Lacámara
Piñata Books, 2010
2010–2011 Tejas Star Book Award

This updated version of the Gingerbread Man story is a complete delight. The piggy cookie jumps off the tray and sets off on a race through a Latino neighborhood, past shops and people and local landmarks. Each encounter with the various characters up and down the street is met with the repeated refrain "Chase me! Chase me down the street! But this is one piggy you won't get to eat! I ran away from the others and I'll run away from you!" The Runaway Piggy is successful at dodging all attempts to catch him . . . until he meets Rosa.

This book lends itself to two ideas for writing: (1) Have students create a new refrain for the Runaway Piggy that has a fluent sound and fits the character's voice, and (2) note the recipes for gingerbread pig cookies at the back of the book and ask students to bring in favorite recipes from home and write them out with bulleted lines and phrases as shown in the mentor text. Or, if you can—do both! (SF, C)

Sonia Sotomayor: A Judge Grows in the Bronx/
La juez que creció en el Bronx
Written by Jonah Winter
Illustrated by Edel Rodriguez
Atheneum Books for Young Readers, 2009
A Children's Book-of-the-Month Featured Selection

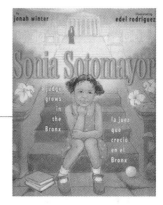

As the first Latina Supreme Court justice, Sonia Sotomayor inspires young and old alike with her determination to do great things despite the odds against her. Readers will appreciate the positive and affirming role of Sonia's mother, who set Sonia on a path of determination to become everything she dreamed of—and more. Sonia's inner strength and values, her love of learning, and her bravery are showcased in this motivating text. This bilingual biography not only has a powerful message, its sentence fluency also shines and makes for a beautiful read-aloud.

After reading aloud and discussing the book as a class, have students go back through and note the different ways in which Jonah Winter, the author, began his sentences. Make a list of the different sentence beginnings and types of sentences, and then challenge students to write a paragraph about a hero they admire, using different sentence types with different sentence beginnings. (SF, I)

Talking with Mother Earth: Poems/Hablando con madre tierra: poemas
Written by Jorge Argueta
Illustrated by Lucía Angela Pérez
Groundwood Books, 2006

Powerful bilingual poems by Salvadoran poet Jorge Argueta explore his heritage and his respect for all the natural elements of life. Argueta, a member of the Nahuatl tribe, uses his poetry to describe the racism he and his people experience. Through his poetry, Jorge embraces his heritage and comes to realize how special and beautiful he is and the sacred connection he feels to his tribe.

Poetry can be an excellent format with which to teach sentence fluency. Have students pick a favorite poem from the book and note the rhythm and flow of each line. Note how dialogue is mixed into the running text. Challenge students to write a two-stanza poem that sounds fluent and shares an important message about a natural element. (SF, I)

Tito Puente: Mambo King/Rey del mambo
Written by Monica Brown
Illustrated by Rafael López
Rayo, 2013
Pura Belpré Honor Book

This energetic, bilingual biography pounds with sounds, syllables, and rhythm to recount the life of Tito Puente, the mambo king. Told simply but with high energy that makes readers feel like tapping their toes, the story is bound to inspire readers to follow their own dreams to success.

As you read the book aloud, have students sway and tap to the tempo and cadence of the sounds. Remind them that sentences should not only be correct but should flow, too, just like music and dancing. When you are finished reading, ask students to tell you how this book is like writing fluently, and post their responses on an anchor chart for sentence fluency. (SF, V)

The Upside Down Boy: El niño de cabeza
Written by Juan Felipe Herrera
Illustrated by Elizabeth Gómez
Lee and Low Books, 2000

It is hard to start school in a new place, and dealing with a new language can make it feel overwhelming. All of the new sounds and routines make Juan feel upside down at times. One day at a time, through singing and poetry, Juan learns English words. His teacher asks him to write a poem, and he's amazed at the result: "I think of Mama, squeeze my pencil, pour letters from the shiny tip like a skinny river" (24). This beautifully poetic bilingual book should be in every classroom library to inspire learners of all ages to appreciate the power that words and writing bring into our lives.

Ask students to write a poem expressing how they think they would feel if they woke up in the morning and found themselves heading to a school where no one spoke their language. Show them the fluent and poignant passages from *The Upside Down Boy* as a model to follow. (SF, I)

Mentor Texts for the Sentence Fluency Trait: Chapter Books

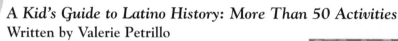

A Kid's Guide to Latino History: More Than 50 Activities
Written by Valerie Petrillo
Chicago Review, 2009

You can create your own special Día celebration to promote reading and writing and to honor Latino culture. Invite people of all ages to participate in the event, and showcase Spanish and English-language books that feature Latino characters in the United States.

At your Día celebration, you can also enjoy Latino foods such as tortillas and salsa, tropical drinks, plantain chips, and chicharrones *(pork rinds); listen to Latino music; and participate in activities to celebrate the day.*

- *Create a mural. Use markers to draw scenes from a book onto white paper. Tape your mural to a wall for the day.*
- *Make paper bag piñatas. Decorate paper lunch bags, and then fill them with tiny toys, candies, and confetti. Use brightly colored ribbon to tie the bags.*
- *Write out and put on a bilingual play based on one of the books featured at your celebration.*
- *Host a reading circle. Take turns reading aloud from a book that is featured at your celebration.* (199)

This book is an overview of the many differences and similarities among Latino groups based on history and geography. You could dip in and out of this treasure chest—chockfull of details about geography, food, culture, language, and just about anything you might want to know about Latino history—to find information, games, and activities that celebrate and honor Latino heritage. Main chapters focus on the following broad topics:

Discovery of the New World
The Spanish North American Frontier
Frontier Life in the Mexican Southwest
Mexican Americans
Puerto Ricans on the Mainland
Cuban Americans
Central Americans
Dominican Americans
South Americans
Latinos: Past, Present, and Future

The excerpted passage offers ideas for a *Diá* celebration of all Latino cultures. I particularly like the suggestion of writing a bilingual play based on one of the books from this resource. Plays are an excellent format in which kids can practice sentence fluency, because a play should be read aloud. Or, if writing a play is too broad in scope, have students create poems as invitations to give to parents, family, neighbors, and other interested community members who might attend the celebration. (SF, I, O)

Enchanted Air: Two Cultures, Two Wings: A Memoir
Written by Margarita Engle
Illustrated by Edel Rodriguez
Atheneum Books for Young Readers, 2015
2015 Pura Belpré Author Award

Refuge
*The ugliness of war photos
and the uncertainty of TV news
join the memory of FBI questions
to make me feel like climbing into
my own secret world.*

*Books are enchanted. Books help me travel.
Books help me breathe.*

*When I climb a tree, I take a book with me.
When I walk home from school, I carry
my own poems, inside my mind,
where no one else
can reach the words
that are entirely
completely
forever
mine.* (54)

Ah and *awe*—two words I felt when reading *Enchanted Air*. The writing is magnificent, drawing the reader into every page, every image, every imaginable emotion of Engle's childhood—torn between two worlds in the Cold War struggle between Cuba and the United States. Her achingly beautiful introspection shows us a loved but lonely young writer experiencing a confusing and often terrifying world.

The poem "Refuge" is a favorite because reading books can be the way all young people cope with complicated lives. The beginning of the poem could easily reflect the nightly news today, not just fifty years ago. Ask students to note the way each poem captures a moment, a snippet of thought—in this case the war and how she retreats into books, where she can live unafraid. Work with students to read the poem aloud as a choral reading so they can hear the rhythm and cadence of the piece, noting where lines start and stop. Have students write about a concern of their own and what they do to manage it in a free-verse poem, as Engle's piece models so well. (SF, I)

The Lightning Dreamer: Cuba's Greatest Abolitionist
Written by Margarita Engle
Houghton Mifflin Harcourt, 2013
Pura Belpré Honor Book, 2014 PEN Literary Award for Best Young Adult Book, VOYA Top Shelf for Middle School Readers 2013 list, 2014 International Latino Book Award Honorable Mention, NCTE Notable Book for the Language Arts, ALSC Notable Children's Book for 2013, YALSA 2014 Best Fiction for Young Adults

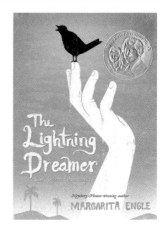

"Tula"
Opinions.
Ideas.
Possibilities.
So many!
How can I choose?
Between bursts
of lightning-swift energy,
I enjoy peaceful moments
when the whole world
seems to be a flowing river
of verse
and all I have to do is learn
how to swim.

During those times,
I find it so easy to forget

that I'm just a girl who is expected
to live
Without thoughts. (41)

Readers will immediately connect with the voice of Gertrudis Gómez de Avellaneda, nicknamed Tula, a young girl in nineteenth-century Cuba who narrates this story. Tula bravely resists an arranged marriage (at age fourteen) and uses language, specifically her poems, to fight against the injustices of her time. She dares to write about what is forbidden—standing up for the rights of those who have no rights, for the unseen, the poor, the unborn. This is a sophisticated text written in free-verse poetry. It is my favorite of all the books I read while creating this resource, but students will need historical context and background (provided in the book) to understand the multilayered concepts conveyed in the eloquence of the pages.

Every page of this brilliant book contains profound and fluent passages that will inspire writers. If you use the one excerpted here, focus on its striking fluency. Note that it has been written as free-verse poetry but is easily read as sentences. The book can be a launching place for research on women's rights and human rights. It can also be a model for how to write fluently, using phrases and words that linger in the mind long after they are read. (SF, I)

Portraits of Hispanic American Heroes
Written by Juan Felipe Herrerra
Paintings by Raúl Colón
Dial Books for Young Readers, 2014

Sample quotes by heroes from the book:

"We will win." Adelina Otero-Warren (18)

"Democracy must belong to us all." Dennis "Dionisio"
Chavez (26)

"I was my own road." Julia De Burgos (34)

"Since I was very young I have always worked hard at whatever I have had to
do." Desi Arnaz (38)

"I travel around, planting an idea." César Estrada Chávez (42)

"I hope I'll see in my lifetime a growing realization that we are one world."
Helen Rodriguez-Trias (46)

"¡Sí, se peude! Yes, we can!" Dolores Huerta (50)

"There were no role models. I was my own role model—myself." Rita Moreno
(58)

"If you have a chance to help others and fail to do so, you're wasting your time on this earth." Roberto Clemente (62)

"I believe a good education can take you anywhere on earth and beyond." Ellen Ochoa (82)

Magnificently written and illustrated, this book contains short biographical sketches of twenty Latino men and women who have been instrumental in the arts, politics, the sciences, athletics, and humanitarian efforts. This collection serves as an excellent model of how to express the essence of a person's life and his or her contributions in a few short, lyrical, power-packed sentences.

Show students the table of contents and help them select a person they want to know more about. Working with a small group, ask students to read the passage about their person and discuss why the person was included in the book as a hero. Ask them to take note of the quotations in the text that capture a key belief, quote, or core value for each hero and have them share their opinion about what it means and how it relates to the hero's life. Tell them to write short, power-packed, lyrical, effective sentences for their opinion pieces. Don't miss the sestina for Victoria Leigh Soto, beloved first-grade teacher killed at Sandy Hook Elementary School in Newtown, Connecticut, on December 14, 2012. (SF, I, V)

The Smoking Mirror (Garza Twins, Volume 1)
Written by David Bowles
IFWG, 2015
2015 Pura Belpré Honor Book

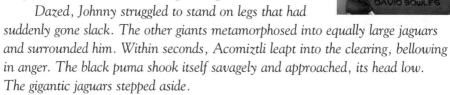

Then he emerged into a circular clearing, ringed by stunted trees and high dunes. In the middle, a dozen giants stood waiting. As he scrambled to slow down and avoid them, one shifted before his eyes, becoming a massive jaguar. Its right forepaw, the size of Johnny's entire body, slammed into him, hurling him against a dune.

Dazed, Johnny struggled to stand on legs that had suddenly gone slack. The other giants metamorphosed into equally large jaguars and surrounded him. Within seconds, Acomiztli leapt into the clearing, bellowing in anger. The black puma shook itself savagely and approached, its head low. The gigantic jaguars stepped aside.

Oh, no. (88)

Reviewers call this book the Latino Percy Jackson, a perfect description of a text that will, without question, become a favorite of young readers. It's the first in a series about twelve-year-old twins Carol and Johnny Garza, whose lives are upended when their mother disappears and their father sends them to Mexico. Little do they know that they are *naguals*, or shape shifters, a magical power inherited from their mother. The high-energy story moves quickly as Carol and Johnny face dangerous adventures in the Aztec underworld.

As with any well-written chapter book, the possibilities for writing inspiration as a mentor text are endless. However, I was struck by how easily the sentences flowed, as the excerpt above illustrates, and how quickly I was drawn into the action because of the artfully crafted sentences. Ask students to add a short paragraph after "Oh, no" that includes Johnny's internal or external dialogue at this point. It should flow logically into the next passage where Acomiztli speaks. This would make a good activity for reinforcing the voice trait, too. (SF, V)

Under the Mambo Moon
Written by Julia Durango
Illustrated by Fabricio VandenBroeck
Charlesbridge, 2011
Texas Bluebonnet Master List 2012–2013

Dr. Solís

Just as the bomba *drummers*
call to each other,
challenging the dances
to reply,
a salty Puerto Rican breeze
wends its way north
and whispers in my ear.

And just like the dancers
who answer the call,
heeding the summons
of the beating drums,
an old man becomes
young again and remembers
his island home. (11)

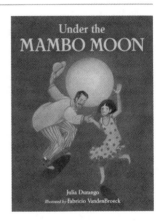

We can dance our way through the pages of this picture book that features the musical heritage of Latin America. Its simple story line, told in English with a few Spanish words, takes place in Papi's music store on a summer night. In a stunning collection of poems detailing the memories of different characters about their homelands, readers are treated to insights about the sizzle and sway of dance rhythms such as merengue, salsa, and samba.

Poetry as musically written as Durango's can inspire students to write elegant phrases and sentences. Invite students to select words and phrases from one or two poems they particularly like and weave those words into a poem of their own, focusing on something musical they know or have learned about dance from this lyrical text. (SF, WC)

THE AUTHOR AND READER AS TRAVELERS
By Margarita Engle

I feel fortunate to live in a time and place where the rich traditions of Latin American poetry can influence US Latino children's literature.

Gertrudis Gómez de Avellaneda was one of the nineteenth century's greatest writers and one of the world's earliest feminist authors. She wrote Latin America's first abolitionist novel, an interracial romance published more than a decade before *Uncle Tom's Cabin*. When I decided to write *The Lightning Dreamer*, I made an effort to depict her childhood and youth in a way that might feel like time travel. I used present tense and multiple voices, hoping to introduce a sense of immediacy and participation. Verse novels offer young readers an interactive experience. Poems can be performed as reader's theater, or children can write their own poems in other voices, to present additional points of view.

Most of my books are inspired by historical figures who found hope in situations that must have seemed hopeless. I chose these stories because I feel that the themes of freedom and peace are just as relevant today as they were long ago.

In the case of my verse memoir, *Enchanted Air, Two Cultures, Two Wings*, I traveled only as far back in time as my own childhood, but the feeling was still one of leaping back into the Cold War. A memoir written in present tense might be unusual, but it is faithful to the nature of memory, which is always intense, as if the events and emotions are still occurring. Writing about my childhood meant visiting those memories. Many were painful. I grew up Cuban American in California, spent summers with my extended family on the island, and then lost the right to travel after US-Cuban diplomatic relations broke down. In my daily life I tend to be timid and cautious, but writing *Enchanted Air* required boldness. I had to write as if I didn't care what adults think. I had to write with children in mind, children who can't imagine two countries staying mad at each other for more than fifty years, children who are the only possible peacemakers of the future.

People often ask why I write my stories in verse instead of traditional prose. I've thought about it a lot over the years, and the answer is simple. Poetry makes me happy. Even when I write about difficult subjects, I find solace in the beauty of language. Poetry allows me to write from the heart, building a home for complex emotions.

My hope is that young readers will feel inspired to write their own verses, bringing new thoughts and feelings into the breaks between stanzas and the pauses between poems. All I can do is plant a small garden and let readers grow it into a world. Whenever teachers send me verses written by their students in response to mine, I know that I've met my goal of communicating with the future by visiting the past. ◉

Chapter 7

THE CURMUDGEON

CONVENTIONS

W e edit for conventions because we care about our reader. Whether our reader is a teacher, a peer, a family member, a friend, or the general public, we want him or her to be able to follow our writing effortlessly and become immersed in our ideas. That can happen only if our reader is not bogged down by unintentional errors in the writing.

Conventions are the editing standards we apply to a piece of writing to make it mechanically correct and, therefore, easy to read: spelling, capitalization, punctuation, paragraphing, and grammar and usage. The conventions trait may seem like old hat, but it's an important trait because it influences the writing as a whole and affects how successfully the other traits come across to the reader. Each of these conventions has its own set of rules—similar to the rules a copy editor follows to prepare text for publication—which must be taught so students can apply them with accuracy and consistency to their writing. Whether it's deciding where to stop or start a sentence, setting off what words are being said aloud, discerning proper nouns from common nouns, spelling familiar and unfamiliar words correctly, or one of the many other considerations that the conventions trait presents, we need conventions to make meaning clear. Period. (Or is that an exclamation mark?) Perhaps this makes me a conventions geek, but I freely admit to playing around with conventions when I write to "capitalize" on voice, "punctuate" the idea, and create sentences that challenge the "conventional" wisdom.

There are standard conventions to which we must adhere, unless we depart from them for a clear purpose. To show strength in conventions, the writer must skillfully and confidently apply these key qualities:

- **Checking Spelling:** Spelling well includes the correct use of sight words, high-frequency words, and even less-familiar words. Unless intentionally misspelled for voice or other literary purposes, the spelling is accurate throughout.
- **Punctuating Effectively and Paragraphing Accurately:** Basic punctuation skills and creative use of punctuation to highlight the meaning and the message is evident. The text is broken into paragraphs in the right places to show subtle shifts in the development of the idea.
- **Capitalizing Correctly:** The use of capital letters shows an in-depth understanding of how to capitalize writing elements such as abbreviations, proper names, and titles. Capitalization is used correctly and consistently throughout on basic elements: the beginning of sentences, the pronoun *I*, and so on.
- **Applying Grammar and Usage:** Words and their prefixes and suffixes have been combined to form grammatically correct phrases and sentences. There is consistent use of correct grammar and usage, unless standard English rules are broken for stylistic effect.

The Traits Dinner Party: Conventions

Like the grumpy old uncle whom everyone loves *and* hates, Conventions cozies up to the other dinner guests, taking in every word, every nuance—almost as though he is waiting to catch someone in a misstatement or a mistake. He harrumphs and guffaws to punctuate the conversation but doesn't add significant content. Rather, he's satisfied to demand clarification now and again, then nod wisely in approval or shake his head in contempt.

Although generally a traditionalist, Conventions has been known to show an edgier side now and again. Tonight, for instance, he is wearing his pilot's black jacket with captain's stripes on the sleeves, a crisp white shirt, and a black tie—his pride-and-joy uniform before retiring from the airlines—with denim jeans. His sense of importance can get on everyone's nerves, though. Case in point: as dinner is served, Conventions takes his place at the foot of the table, opposite Ideas at the head, which makes other guests bristle ("Who does he think *he* is?" whispers Word Choice conspiratorially to Voice). Ideas is unruffled by this seating arrangement, however, knowing that Conventions often feels undervalued by the others; this time she wants him to feel welcome and important.

As dinner is served, Conventions notes that Organization has made a place-setting faux pas, placing only one teaspoon per setting instead of the standard two. He comments that Word Choice should settle down before the meal gets cold and that Sentence Fluency should sit up straighter. Voice grimaces and tries to smooth things over with the others. Everyone understands that Conventions is a curmudgeon and a bit of a stickler, but these kinds of comments don't endear him to the group. The lighter side of Conventions doesn't show up until after dinner, when his piano accompaniment to Sentence Fluency's dance progresses into more popular tunes, ending with all the traits friends on their feet, singing and swaying to "Stand by Me."

Choosing Mentor Texts for the Conventions Trait

You can use almost any book as a model for great use of conventions because they have been through the full writing process with editors, copy editors, and proofreaders all applying conventions with the author's input as well. Often you'll find books that showcase other traits but stand out as great models for interesting use of or attention to standard conventions of writing as well. Those are the ones you want to share with students—the books they love first for other characteristics, then come back to for a closer look through the conventions lens. Here are some questions you might ask yourself when considering a particular book to model the conventions trait:

Checking Spelling: Are the interesting words in the text challenging to spell? Did the author take liberties to try new words and, therefore, new spellings? Are there high-frequency words in the book that students could see in a new context?

Punctuating Effectively and Paragraphing Accurately: Where are examples of basic punctuation used well (end punctuation, commas, quotation marks)? How is end punctuation handled differently in Spanish from how it's handled in English? Is there evidence of a more sophisticated use of punctuation (ellipses, dashes, colons, semicolons)? What is the logic behind how the piece is paragraphed?

Capitalizing Correctly: Does the text respect the rules of standard capitalization? Does the text break the rules of standard capitalization, and if so, where? Has the author used capitalization to create voice or emphasize key points?

Applying Grammar and Usage: What percentage of the text uses Standard English grammar? What percentage takes risks and breaks traditional rules for effect? Are there specific examples of grammar principles that you can exemplify and showcase for students (such as pronoun/noun antecedent agreement, tense and tense shift, or homophones)?

Conventions Convention: Getting a Handle on Conventions

Third graders have it all figured out: all we need to master conventions is to elevate each to superhero status—behold, Lowercase Man (Figure 7.1)! Just imagine the series of superheroes these kids could create and write about. Then it's important to have a convention of conventions and sort out the rules of procedures. Clever and fun.

Even with the most creative ideas at our fingertips, however, conventions can be a difficult area to teach and to learn. The English language is fraught with exceptions to every rule. Ask anyone who has tried to spell *believe, definitely, fiery, receipt, vacuum, weird,* and *misspell*—along with a host of others. Punctuation and capitalization are more consistent and follow the rules more systematically, but grammar gives us fits as well. So many rules to learn—so many times they are broken in order to be right. No wonder kids are confused.

My best suggestion for working with conventions is to enter into a partnership with students. So much of the time it's the teacher doing the editing, marking the papers, making the changes. We need students to learn how to do this for themselves, beginning with the simplest of editing tasks. Start slowly and build toward independence—practicing what we have learned as "gradual release of responsibility" (Pearson and Gallagher 1983).

Figure 7.1 Clever third graders had a creative experience bringing the conventions trait to life: Lowercase Man is on his way to a conventions convention, battling the evil purveyors of faulty capitalization everywhere.

Here's how it could go: start with a list of "I can" rules, or, if you teach in the older grades, "No excuses." These have to be super simple, because you are going to note whether they are used in student writing on the fly, as you work the room, not when you take a set of papers home to read in depth. Try these to begin:

1. Always spell _____ correctly.
   Choose a word that really bugs you when you see it on student papers because you know the student can spell it, but he or she has not caught the problem word before the paper was turned in.
2. Always have punctuation at the end of the sentence.
   Or, if you want to include writing in Spanish, "the beginning and end of the sentence."
3. Always capitalize the first word in the sentence. Or: always capitalize the pronoun *I*.
   One or the other, but not both as you get started—keep it simple.

4. Always have a subject and verb.
   Or use another fairly straightforward grammar rule that you can easily monitor.

Craft an anchor chart with your students, and post it around the classroom. When you work on an anchor chart together as a class, you cement the ideas and give students increased ownership of their learning. Also handy: you can snap a photo of the chart and print it so students each have a copy to keep for reference in their writing notebooks or folders. During independent writing time, if you notice kids missing any of the items on the chart, remind them kindly to be sure to edit their work before they turn it in. This can give you an idea, too, of what needs to be reviewed as a class or what might be discussed in a small-group or individual writing conference.

Pick one convention at a time to focus on in writing conferences, so as not to overwhelm your young writers; again, use the class chart as a guide. And, if final writing pieces make it to your desk before you notice convention errors, politely hand the papers back and ask students to edit them to be as clear as possible before you read them—because you are very much looking forward to reading their work.

Most teachers I know agree that if they could automatize editing so students knew what to look for first and fix it before it reaches them, writing-teacher life would be a lot smoother. Given that there are hundreds of conventions for student writers to learn, begin with them owning part of the editing process, which in turn will allow you to teach new spelling, punctuation, capitalization, and grammar rules and techniques to help make their writing reader-ready.

EXPLORING LATINO LITERATURE WITH A WRITER'S EYE
By Yuyi Morales

Libros! When I was a kid growing up in Mexico, there were two kinds of *libros* to be found in the shelves of our house: my parents' books and the children's encyclopedia that my mother bought from a door-to-door salesman. My mother reminds me that when I finished reading all the volumes of the encyclopedia I asked her to buy another one, and she was dismayed because she was still making payments on the one we had. I loved reading, but most of the books available for me were not for children or were not narrative books. Instead, I read comic magazines, pamphlets, coloring books, and a few translations of Disney movies. It wasn't until I came to the USA as a new mother that I saw children's books for the first time. I immediately fell in love with them! In much the same way children do, I entered the new experience of learning how to read in English through the world of picture books.

There was something else in books that caught me by surprise: if I looked hard among the shelves of the public library (a search that was less fruitful, but still possible, in the shelves of my local bookstore), I could find books that depicted people, children, and even animals who lived in the Mexican culture that was familiar to me. I was in awe! The protagonists of these books were people who looked like me, who dressed like me, who ate what I ate, and played and sang and dreamed in Spanish like me. I began to develop a new sense of pride and value, and right away I wanted more books like those—and more of that eruption of feelings that came every time I found a book on the shelves that celebrated people like me and my son.

It is with such a fire that I make children's books. May you, reader, one day look on the shelves of your public library and find volcanoes of pride and joy inside many, many books. ➒

Teaching with Mentor Texts for the Conventions Trait

You'll notice that the rest of this chapter is organized differently from the others in this book. Because strong examples of conventions can be gleaned from all books, I will spotlight a few mentor texts that work especially well for teaching conventions; then I'll focus on activities that you can use to teach conventions in lively, engaging ways. What's nice about these activities is that you can use them with just about any book, even ones you've already focused on to teach another trait. (In fact, sometimes that's most effective—to go back through a familiar text to look closely at its use of conventions.)

Biblioburro: A True Story from Colombia/
Biblioburro: Una historia real de Colombia
Written and illustrated by Jeanette Winter
Scholastic, 2010

A delightful true tale of Luis and his love of books! His journey to share books with people who may be less fortunate turns into a tale of fulfilling small yet meaningful dreams. The book has a charming quality, similar to other books by Winter, that students will surely enjoy.

This text is a great example of conventions being used to make the idea stand out in a clear, concise way. Have students examine the use of quotation marks, semicolons, commas, and exclamation marks. Choose one of the passages of dialogue and remove all the punctuation. Then have students add it back in so it makes sense and guides the reader through the sentences. (C, SF)

Fire! ¡Fuego! Brave Bomberos
Written by Susan Middleton Elya
Illustrated by Dan Santat
Bloomsbury, 2012

House fire! And off go the *bomberos* to save the day. In this rollicking rhyming story infused with many Spanish words, readers gain an appreciation for the difficult, dangerous work that firefighters do to keep the community safe.

This book provides a fun opportunity to explore conventions and their relationship to sentence fluency. Go through the book and make a list of the sound words and notice how they are spelled and punctuated. Then have students make up their own sound words and figure out how they would be spelled and capitalized. Ask them to add punctuation in English and Spanish. For example, *¿Bazam? ¡BAZAM!* (C, SF)

José! Born to Dance
Written by Susanna Reich
Illustrated by Raúl Colón
Simon and Schuster Books for Young Readers, 2005

José had a hard time fitting in as a young man. Fiercely determined, he used all the challenges in his life to find his calling: dancing. This gorgeous English book with Spanish words is a sensory explosion of expressions and feelings that move readers to empathize with José and rejoice in his success.

Woven throughout this biography are many sound words and expressive words in both English and Spanish. Discuss the use of interjections with students and how they are punctuated to stand out. Have students find a place in the text where they could add an interjection in English and Spanish, and help them punctuate it correctly in both languages. Or, have them take a look at a piece of writing they're working on and play with adding an interjection in an appropriate spot. (C, V, WC)

Magdalena's Picnic/El picnic de Magdalena
Written by Patricia Aguilar Morrissey
Illustrated by Gretchen Deahl
Red Heart Books, 2014

Magdalena's Picnic is a simply told story of an imagined picnic in the Amazon jungle. Her purple friend, the tapir, accompanies Magdalena as she narrowly escapes jungle dangers to find the perfect picnic spot. This book introduces students to animals and the Amazon jungle environment, including in a detailed author's note at the end, and models simple sentences with complex dialogue punctuation throughout.

Ask students to expand the role of the little brother by adding dialogue to the story. Have them give him a name and provide his reactions to the different threatening events that happen in the story. (C, I)

Activities for Teaching Conventions with Picture Books

Conventions is a trait you can dive into with any picture book. Rather than highlighting more specific book examples, what follows are some teaching ideas, grouped by key quality, which you can apply to favorite books when teaching aspects of the conventions trait.

Checking Spelling

Check It Out
Ask student to fold a blank piece of paper in a hot-dog fold, lengthwise. Select a passage from one of the mentor texts that has a mix of challenging words and everyday words. As you read this section aloud, have students write down on the left side of the paper any words that they think are challenging to spell; on the right side, they can write any words they feel comfortable spelling correctly. Tell them to try for at least seven of each. Compare their spellings with those in the book. If students wish, they can add the words that give them the most trouble to a personal spelling list for reference later.

Ring-a-Ding Spelling
Every week, target a high-frequency word that students sometimes misspell in their writing. (Every teacher has pet peeves—start with one of those. Mine is *a lot* spelled as one word.) As you read a mentor text aloud, ask

students to be aware of the spelling demon word. When someone hears it aloud, he or she can race to the front of the class and ring a bell. Or, kids can make a sound that you predetermine whenever they hear the word. Then, ask the ring-a-ding student to point out the word on the page using a document camera, and ask the class to spell it aloud as a group.

Spell-Checker Is Your Friend

As students use more and more technology in their writing, make sure they know how to use the spell checker option. Try using spell-checker on words in the text that are challenging to spell. Call them out and have students try spelling them using word-processing software. If the word is spelled incorrectly, the software will indicate it—usually with a red squiggly line underneath. Show students how to find the correct spelling, and note that if the incorrect spelling is far from the correct spelling, it may not show up at all in the spell-checker option. If that's the case, have students try typing the word into Google or another search engine and see if it pops up there.

The Word Knows

Ask students to pick a word from a mentor text that they have trouble spelling. Tell them to become that word and write a short piece about how it feels to be spelled incorrectly all the time. Tell students to try to use the word many times in their writing and to use lots of voice to be sure the reader understands the word's position.

Punctuating Effectively and Paragraphing Accurately

Does It Work?

Show students an example of a mentor text that uses punctuation marks at the beginning of the sentence, not just at the end. Explain that in Spanish, end-of-the-sentence punctuation is handled differently from English, and invite their opinions about whether this practice helps them as readers. Ask students to work in groups of four—two for and two against the practice—and create an argument to support their opinion to present to the class.

Outta Here

Retype a passage from the book, leaving out all the punctuation marks. Read the passage aloud exactly as it is newly edited. Give students the unpunctuated version of the text and ask them to work with a partner to add the punctuation back in. Then compare the original book with their edited copies and see how many errors they were able to spot and correct.

Air Quotes

Preselect a passage that has dialogue, and read it aloud. Ask students to use air quotes when they hear dialogue begin and end. Then show them the passage on the document camera and compare their air quotes with those in the edited text.

Paragraph Shift

Give students different mentor texts to study, focusing on how new paragraphs are indicated. Ask them to make a list of the different methods the writer uses to let the reader know a new paragraph is about to start. Make sure students understand that although they will see many paragraphs indented, they will notice other techniques as well (skip a line and left-justify, first paragraph in a section left-justified and the rest indented, indentations for dialogue, and others). Make an anchor chart together showing how to indent paragraphs, and hang it up to use as a guide in student writing.

Capitalizing Correctly

Snaps for Caps

Pick out a section of one of the mentor texts that shows sophisticated use of capitalization, perhaps an abbreviation or an acronym. Before you read this passage aloud, tell students to snap their fingers any time they think there should be a capital letter. Have them compare their choices with the original text by displaying the text using a document camera. Discuss any uses of capitals kids were sure about and also any that made them wonder, and talk about the rules that guide each example.

Take It Out/Put It In

Divide the class into small groups. Give each a short passage from the mentor text and ask them to rewrite it without any capitalization. Then have them trade passages with another group, who will now add the capitalization back in. Check their final choices against the original text.

Sweet Tweet

Have students create a tweet to the author of one of their favorite mentor texts without using any capital letters. Ask them how comfortable they feel sending the tweet or if they think it should be edited for capitals first. Discuss the difference between the two versions, and ask students if it is appropriate to leave out capitals or important to include them in messages to people they don't know, and why.

An Air of En-title-ment

Show students the titles of several mentor texts and point out how the words are capitalized. Ask students to work with a partner and write a short set of capitalization rules that apply to titles: the first word and last word are always capitalized; nouns, verbs, adjectives, and adverbs are the only words capitalized; prepositions, articles, and conjunctions aren't usually capitalized (unless they're the first word). If students don't know these specific rules, see if they can infer them by the examples. This is a great opportunity to reemphasize parts of speech and how they are used in the titles.

Applying Grammar and Usage

Make It and Break It

Find a model sentence in one of the mentor texts that is constructed with Standard English and can serve as a model of grammar and usage rules your students struggle with, such as pronoun/noun antecedents, plurals/possessives, or change of verb tense. Ask students to name specific grammar rules and examples that indicate how the sentence was correctly constructed. Then, have students rewrite the sentence so it intentionally breaks the rules. Have them read both sentences aloud to a partner and comment about which sounds better and why.

To Adverb or Not

Show students a passage from a mentor text that uses several adverbs. Ask them to identify the role of the adverb—to modify the verb—in the sentences. See if students can eliminate any of the adverbs by choosing a different verb. For example, instead of *run slowly* they might come up with *amble*, *stroll*, or *saunter*. Ask students to decide which is more effective: the sentence with the adverb or the one with the new verb in its place.

Amazing Appositives

Find a short, declarative sentence in one of the mentor texts that has at least two nouns. For example, *Diego showed me his muddy soccer cleats*. Ask students to write it on a paper and hand it to a partner. Then, have the partner add an appositive, which is a noun or a pronoun phrase that renames another noun or pronoun in some way, to the sentence. New sentence example: *Diego, <u>my best friend</u>, showed me his muddy soccer cleats*. Then, punctuate the sentence together, if needed, and add an additional appositive, such as this: *Diego, <u>my best friend</u>, showed me his muddy soccer cleats, <u>an essential piece of equipment for playing well</u>*. Discuss the role of appositives in the mentor texts where you find them.

Super Superlatives

Using an example of a word from a mentor text, show students how to change a suffix to give the word a different weight of importance: *big, bigger, biggest; yummy, yummier, yummiest*. Have them look through the pages of other books and find examples of words that can be made into comparatives and superlatives, too, and write them on sticky notes, then place the notes on the page with the original text. They can go back into their own writing to look for comparatives and superlatives as well.

What makes the old curmudgeon conventions fun to teach is that you can use just about any book as a mentor text, and kids can really have fun playing with rules and words and language. They can start applying what they're learning to their own writing. And soon they'll start to see how conventions really help all the other traits shine, in much the same way as our Conventions dinner guest leads his friends in "Stand by Me" at the end of the evening: he seems nitpicky and hard to please, but in the end, he just wants them to sing together in harmony. Mastery of the conventions trait, in other words, helps our young writers convey their brilliant ideas, organization, voice, words, and sentence fluency in the best possible ways—much to their readers' benefit.

I'm betting all my exclamation marks that every reader of this book would love a cache of new, creative ideas for teaching conventions. And wouldn't we have fun learning from one another? Please share your ideas on social media using my Twitter handle @writingthief or the hashtag #dreamwakers to add book titles and ideas for teaching conventions so everyone can grow their teaching idea bank.

WHY'S A GAL LIKE ME WRITING BOOKS WITH SPANISH?
By Susan Elya

My path to being an author of picture books with Spanish has been a winding one. It started back in Iowa with my dad, who brought home a Spanish dictionary pamphlet from the printing company where he was a pressman. Since we had few books in our home and this was the first one with foreign words in it, my siblings and I were intrigued. My older sister was taking Spanish in high school, and I also signed up so I could join their conversation around the dinner table.

Señor Bretos was from Cuba. So were most of my other Iowa Spanish teachers. After graduating from high school I went to Mexico with my teacher and thirty other kids. It was my first time on an airplane and my first time out of the United States. I couldn't believe a whole country spoke the language I'd been studying for four years.

I kept taking Spanish classes at Iowa State University, along with my elementary education courses. Not many Iowans were taking Spanish back then. The whole department was about four professors. I studied abroad in Spain and student-taught in Venezuela.

I graduated with a double degree and a minor in secondary education. When I applied for the third-grade job in Nowhere, Nebraska, in 1977, the principal called and asked if I'd interview for the high school Spanish job instead. I did. I got it. I moved to the cornfields. I taught there two years and took five kids to Mexico in 1981.

Tired of the farm town, I moved to Omaha and got a teaching job in a middle school, where I started the Spanish curriculum. I wrote the softcover textbook that the middle-grade students used for their nine-week course. Five and a half years later, I taught high school Spanish in the same district, where the program had doubled in size.

From there my marriage took me to San Diego, where I taught native speakers Spanish, and I also taught ESL. *Home at Last* came out of that experience. My family moved to the San Francisco Bay area, and I stayed home for the next twenty years, raising my kids and writing during naptimes. My mom suggested I add Spanish to my stories.

Kids are kids no matter where they are born and no matter what language they grow up with. People are people no matter where they live. Humans have universal experiences regarding friendship, love, feelings, and fears. My job is to help children understand that they have more things in common with children of other cultures than differences.

Yes, I am a weirdo in many ways, and I am still amazed when people won't buy my books because they aren't all in English. The country is changing. The world is changing. We need books that will help bring people together by their common experiences instead of set them apart by their differences. ◉

DREAM WAKERS

FINAL THOUGHTS

My son Sam was not much of a reader. By eighth grade, his reading-addicted mother began to despair. He did what the teacher asked of him but not one thing more, and I often suspected he did less. Oh, how I despised those CliffsNotes and SparkNotes. Thank goodness online resources were not available then. Over the years, I tried to entice Sam with books I thought he'd enjoy—but to no avail. He always smiled and said something sweet like "Thanks, Mom. I'll look at it later." Yeah, right.

One day, I brought home a copy of *The House on Mango Street* and left it on the kitchen counter. It disappeared. I was suspicious about what might have happened to it, so I got another copy and left it hanging around too. It also disappeared. I began to have hope. By the time my little experiment was done, I had "lost" seven copies. As it turns out, one found its way to Chico, one to Tony, one to Jessie, Frankie, Ryan, Jimmi—and Sam. One night while they were playing a video game, I heard them talking about the book and what it meant to each of them—brown, black, and white. I was moved to tears by their insights and personal connections. Behold, the power of books to create bridges across boundaries of culture and language. Diverse texts engage us in a connection to a bigger, worldwide community.

After I lost Sam, I found his copy among his most treasured things—tucked away among Michael Jordan's rookie basketball card, an eclectic music collection, and other childhood memorabilia. *The House on Mango Street* may be *the* book that first got him excited about reading, but it was not the last. By the time he left us, he was a voracious reader with a deep appreciation for humanity, equity, and fairness. Thank you, Sandra Cisneros, for helping to shape the character of my beautiful son, and for awakening the dreams of countless young people and adults who could see themselves in those pages, hear their voices in your words, and imagine their neighbors and friends and family in your stories.

Here is what I believe: every child deserves access to high-quality literature to learn to read and write. I understand that it can be hard—families are not able to buy books, library collections can't grow as quickly as we'd like, funding is not available for teachers to buy books for the classroom in quantities that would affect more of their students. We have to keep trying. For any child, a single book can awaken dreams to enter a different world—a world where some of the characters look like him, where heroes come in all colors and backgrounds, where ideas about what might be possible in her life are limitless.

It's become my passion to put together collections of books I believe students might find interesting, intriguing, and informational on their journey to literacy, books that awaken dreams. I hope many of these books that celebrate Latino life and culture find their way to your classrooms, school libraries, and homes, so readers like Sam and his friends—boys and girls from all backgrounds—can awaken their dreams through the inspiring words and worlds of these magnificent authors.

Here is how I selected these books—a lengthy and fascinating process. First I scoured the Internet for lists of children's books compiled by reputable sources:

1. About.com's Hispanic and Latino Heritage in Books for Children and Teens by Elizabeth Kennedy
   http://childrensbooks.about.com/od/culturalhispanic/tp/hispanic_latino.htm
   From this source I tracked down award-winning, high-quality Latino literature—literature that has won the Pura Belpré Award, the Américas Book Award for Children's and Young Adult Literature, the Tomás Rivera Mexican American Children's Book Award, and other awards that honor Latino literature by category.

2. Celebrating Diverse Latino Cultures, Literature, and Literacy Everyday by Dr. Jamie Naidoo
   www.ala.org/alsc/sites/ala.org.alsc/files/content/confevents/institute/institutehandouts/Diversity%20Handout.pdf
   This is a gold mine of information distributed at the 2010 presentation to the Association of Library Services to Children by Dr. Jamie Naidoo, with links to nine organizations and lists that contain recommended books. I investigated the links, cross-referenced book titles from one recommended list to others, and discovered the books that had been recommended by more than one reliable source.

3. Latino Children's Book Resource
   http://ccb.lis.illinois.edu/Projects/Additions%20on%209-20-07/CCB/CCB/mhommel2/latinoresource.htm
   I also reviewed lists of recommended books from large universities, such as this one from the University of Illinois at Urbana-Champaign, as well as lists from agencies in regions of the country with large populations of Latino students.

4. Amazon.com
www.amazon.com/Childrens-Books
I went to trusty old Amazon.com. I know: researching on Amazon is hardly scientific. But because the website posts reviews from *Booklist, School Library Journal*, and other review sources in which I have faith, I was able to get good information on particular books. And of course, I was excited to see the cover of each book, read a few pages, look at the art, and get a feel for it before hitting that dangerous "Amazon One Click" button!

To each book I considered, I applied a set of criteria to help me determine quality. I developed my criteria based on Naidoo's ideas and also used the thinking from Louise Derman-Sparks's *"Guide for Selecting Anti-Bias Children's Books."* I also consulted another resource: The Children's Literature and Reading Special Interest Group of the International Literacy Association.

Naidoo's evaluation criteria are as follows:

1. Examine the personal traits of the character.
2. Examine the role of various characters.
3. Examine and identify cultural stereotypes.
4. Examine the diversity of presentation in text and illustrations.
5. Examine the experience of the author and illustrator.

The criteria and reflection questions for each are available in their entirety in *Celebrating Cuentos* by Dr. Jamie Naidoo (246–47) or on the PDF from his 2010 presentation to the ALSC (see URL on page 139).

From Derman-Sparks, I reviewed and applied her list of "Ten Quick Ways to Analyze Children's Books for Racism and Sexism."

1. Check the Illustrations for Stereotypes, Tokenism, and Invisibility
2. Check the Story Line and Relationships Between People
3. Look at Messages About Different Lifestyles
4. Consider the Effects on Children's Self- and Social Identities
5. Look for Books About Children and Adults Engaging in Actions for Change
6. Consider the Author's or Illustrator's Background and Perspective
7. Watch for Loaded Words
8. Look at the Copyright Date

9. Assess the Appeal of the Story and Illustrations to Young
   Children
10. Check for Age Appropriateness

Each of the ten tips has an explanation with examples, which I found helpful and enlightening.

Another source for criteria to use in selecting bias-free books is the Children's Literature and Reading Special Interest Group of the International Literacy Association, which selects twenty-five books each year representing the best in diverse literature. The committee looks for the following criteria:

- Richness of detail concerning the group or groups depicted
- An approach that celebrates diversity and the common bonds of humanity
- In-depth treatment of issues
- Depiction of authentic interaction among characters within and across groups
- Inclusion of members of a minority group for purposes other than tokenism
- Thought-provoking content that invites reflection, critical analysis, and response (Ward 2015, 22)

And finally, because I'm a big believer in books and their power to transform lives (including my own), I purchased and read every book I selected for this text. It would be impossible for me to recommend those books to you without touching, feeling, and reading them—several times—myself.

❀ APPENDIX B ❀
BOOKS AND TRAITS AT A GLANCE

The book list that follows contains an alphabetical listing of all the books in *Dream Wakers*. You'll find the page number to locate the books along with key information about them. The chart is divided into two parts: Picture Books and Chapter Books. I selected the trait that is the strongest in each book and marked it with and X. I used an O to indicate a secondary trait. Remember, however, you are free to align the books with the traits of writing however works best for you and your students.

Page	Title	Author	Illustrator	Publisher/Year	Language	Genre: Subcategories	I	O	V	WC	SF	C
Picture Books												
48	*A Is for Activist/ A de activista*	Martha E. Gonzalez	Innosanto Nagara	Triangle Square Press, 2013	English and Spanish editions	Narrative nonfiction		X		O		
49	*Abuelo and the Three Bears/Abuelo y los tres osos*	Jerry Tello	Ana López Escrivá	Scholastic, 1997	Bilingual	Fairy tale		X		O		
49	*Abuela's Weave*	Omar S. Castañada	Enrique O. Sanchez	Lee and Low Books, 1993	English	Biography		X			O	
106	*Action Jackson*	Jan Greenberg and Sandra Jordan	Robert Andrew Parker	Macmillan, 2007	English	Biography			O		X	
27	*The Barking Mouse*	Antonio Sacre	Alfredo Aguirre	Albert Whitman, 2003	English with Spanish words	Magical realism	X			O		
129	*Biblioburro: A True Story from Colombia/ Biblioburro: Una historia real de Colombia*	Jeanette Winter	Jeanette Winter	Scholastic, 2010	English and Spanish editions	Historical fiction					O	X
28	*Black and Blanco! Engaging Art in English y Español*	artekids.org	artekids.org	Trinity University Press, 2013	Bilingual	Narrative nonfiction	X			O		

Picture Books

Page	Title	Author	Illustrator	Publisher/Year	Language	Genre: Subcategories	I	O	V	WC	SF	C
49	Book Fiesta! Celebrate Children's Day/Book Day/Celebremos El día de los niños/El día de los libros	Pat Mora	Rafael López	HarperCollins Children's Books, 2009	Bilingual	Narrative nonfiction	O	X				
50	¡Bravo!	Ginger Foglesong Guy	René King Moreno	Greenwillow Books, 2010	Bilingual	Realistic fiction		X		O		
86	Building on Nature: The Life of Antoni Gaudí	Rachel Rodríguez	Julie Paschkis	Henry Holt, 2009	English	Biography	O			X		
50	Caye Boy: Barefoot Adventures of an Island Child	Jessica Retsick Wigh	Andrew Young	CreateSpace, 2013	English	Realistic fiction		X		O		
106	The Cazuela That the Farm Maiden Stirred	Samantha R. Vamos	Rafael López	Charlesbridge, 2013	English with Spanish words	Narrative nonfiction	O	O		O	X	
51	Cecilia and Miguel Are Best Friends/Cecilia y Miguel son mejores amigos	Diane Gonzales Bertrand	Thelma Muraida	Arte Público, 2014	Bilingual	Realistic fiction	O	X				
51	Chicks and Salsa	Aaron Reynolds	Paulette Bogan	Bloomsbury, 2007	English	Magical realism		X		O		

Picture Books

Page	Title	Author	Illustrator	Publisher/Year	Language	Genre: Subcategories	I	O	V	WC	SF	C
87	Clatter Bash! A Day of the Dead Celebration	Richard Keep	Richard Keep	Peachtree, 2004	English with Spanish words	Narrative nonfiction				X		O
68	The Composition/ La composición	Antonio Skármeta	Alfonso Ruano	Groundwood Books, 1998	English and Spanish editions	Narrative fiction	O		X			
52	Counting on Community	Innosanto Nagara	Innosanto Nagara	Triangle Square, 2015	English	Informational/ board book		X			O	
28	Dalia's Wondrous Hair/ El cabello maravilloso de Dalia	Laura Lacámara (translated by Gabriela Baenza Ventura)	Laura Lacámara	Piñata Books, 2014	Bilingual	Magical realism	X			O		
68	A Day's Work	Eve Bunting	Ronald Himler	Clarion Books, 1994	English	Realistic fiction			X	O		
69	The Dead Family Diaz	P. J. Bracegirdle	Poly Bernatene	Dial Books for Young Readers, 2012	English	Magical realism			X		O	
52	Dear Primo: A Letter to My Cousin	Duncan Tonatiuh	Duncan Tonatiuh	Abrams Books for Young Readers, 2010	English with Spanish words	Realistic fiction	O	X				

Picture Books

Page	Title	Author	Illustrator	Publisher/Year	Language	Genre: Subcategories	I	O	V	WC	SF	C
69	Diego	Jonah Winter (translated by Amy Prince)	Jeanette Winter	Dragonfly Books, 1991	Bilingual	Biography			X	O		
87	Diego Rivera: His World and Ours	Duncan Tonatiuh	Duncan Tonatiuh	Abrams Books for Young Readers, 2011	English	Biography	O			X		
29	Doña Flor: A Tall Tale About a Giant Woman with a Great Big Heart/Doña Flor: Un cuento de una mujer gigante con un gran corazón	Pat Mora	Raúl Colón	Dragonfly Books, 2005	English and Spanish editions	Tall tale	X		O			
107	Drum Dream Girl: How One Girl's Courage Changed Music	Margarita Engle	Rafael López	HMH Books for Young Readers, 2015	English	Nonfiction/ biography/ poetry				O	X	
29	¡El Cucuy! A Bogey Man Cuento in English and Spanish	Joe Hayes	Honorio Robledo	Cinco Puntos, 2001	Bilingual	Folktale	X		O			
53	Elena's Serenade	Campbell Geeslin	Ana Juan	Atheneum Books for Young Readers, 2004	English with Spanish words	Magical realism	O	X				

Picture Books

Page	Title	Author	Illustrator	Publisher/Year	Language	Genre: Subcategories	I	O	V	WC	SF	C
88	Estas manos: Manitas de mi familia/These Hands: My Family's Hands	Samuel Caraballo	Shawn Costello	Arte Público, 2014	Bilingual	Poetry: ode	O			X		
53	¡Fiesta!	Ginger Foglesong Guy	René King Moreno	Greenwillow Books, 2007	Bilingual	Narrative nonfiction	O	X				
130	Fire!/¡Fuego! Brave Bomberos	Susan Middleton Elya	Dan Santat	Bloomsbury, 2012	Bilingual	Narrative nonfiction					O	X
30	Floating on Mama's Song/Flotando en la canción de mamá	Laura Lacámera	Yuyi Morales	Katherine Tegen Books, 2010	Bilingual	Fiction: magical realism	X	O				
88	Frida	Jonah Winter	Ana Juan	Scholastic, 2002	English and Spanish editions	Biography			O	X		
107	Funny Bones: Posada and His Day of the Dead Calaveras	Duncan Tonatiuh	Duncan Tonatiuh	Abrams, 2015	English	Informational		O			X	
54	Gathering the Sun: An Alphabet in Spanish and English	Alma Flor Ada (translated by Rosa Zubizarreta)	Simón Silva	Rayo, 2001	Bilingual	Poetry	X		O			
54	Gazpacho for Nacho	Tracey Kyle	Carolina Farías	Two Lions: Amazon, 2014	English with Spanish words	Narrative fiction	X	O				

Picture Books

Page	Title	Author	Illustrator	Publisher/Year	Language	Genre: Subcategories	I	O	V	WC	SF	C
55	Good Dream, Bad Dream: The World's Heroes Save the Night/Sueño bueno, sueño malo: Los heroes del mundo salvan la noche!	Juan Calle and Serena Valentino	Juan Calle and Serena Valentino	Immedium, 2014	Bilingual	Fiction: magical realism	O	X			X	
108	Gracias/Thanks	Pat Mora (translated by Adriana Domínguez)	John Parra	Lee and Low Books, 2009	Bilingual	Fiction	O					
89	Green Is a Chile Pepper: A Book of Colors	Roseanne Greenfield Thong	John Parra	Chronicle Books, 2014	Bilingual	Narrative nonfiction	O			X		
89	Guacamole: Un poema para cocinar/A Cooking Poem	Jorge Argueta (translated by Elisa Amado)	Margarita Sada	Groundwood Books, 2012	Bilingual	Narrative nonfiction/ poetry				X	O	
30	Hairs and Pelitos	Sandra Cisneros (translated by Liliana Valenzuela)	Terry Ybáñez	Dragonfly Books, 1984	Bilingual	Realistic fiction	X			O		

Page	Title	Author	Illustrator	Publisher/Year	Language	Genre: Subcategories	I	O	V	WC	SF	C
Picture Books												
55	*I Am Latino: The Beauty in Me*	Sandra L. Pinkney	Photographs by Myles C. Pinkney	Hachette Book Group, 2007	English with Spanish words	Narrative nonfiction	O	X				
70	*I Dreamt. . . A Book About Hope*	Gabriela Olmos (translated into English by Elisa Amado)	Manuel Monroy (et al.)	Groundwood Books, 2013	English	Realistic fiction	O		X			
30	*If the Shoe Fits*	Gary Soto	Terry Widener	Putnam Juvenile, 2002	English	Realistic fiction	X		O			
31	*In My Family/ En mi familia*	Carmen Lomas Garza (Spanish translation by Francisco X. Alarcón)	Carmen Lomas Garza	Children's Book Press, 1996	Bilingual	Narrative nonfiction	X			O		
130	*José! Born to Dance*	Susanna Reich	Raúl Colón	Simon and Schuster Books for Young Readers, 2005	English	Biography			O	O		X
55	*Just a Minute: A Trickster Tale and Counting Book*	Yuyi Morales	Yuyi Morales	Chronicle Books, 2003	English	Folklore	O	X				

Picture Books

Page	Title	Author	Illustrator	Publisher/Year	Language	Genre: Subcategories	I	O	V	WC	SF	C
56	Just in Case: A Trickster Tale and Spanish Alphabet Book	Yuyi Morales	Yuyi Morales	Roaring Brook, 2008	English with Spanish words	Folklore	O	X		O		
56	Kikirikí * Quiquiriquí	Diane de Anda (translated by Karina Hernandez)	Daniel Lechón	Piñata Books, 2004	Bilingual	Realistic fiction	O	X				
70	La Mariposa	Francisco Jiménez	Simón Silva	Houghton Mifflin, 1994	English and Spanish editions	Realistic fiction			X	O		
90	Little Roja Riding Hood	Susan Middleton Elya	Susan Guevara	G. P. Putnam's Sons, 2014	English with Spanish words	Fairy tales				X		O
31	The Lizard and the Sun/La lagartija y el sol	Alma Flor Ada	Felipe Dávalos	Dragonfly Books, 2007	Bilingual	Legend	X	O				
131	Magdalena's Picnic: El picnic de Magdalena	Patricia Aguilar Morrissey	Gretchen Deahl	Red Heart Books, 2014	Bilingual	Realistic fiction	O					X
32	A Mango in the Hand: A Story Told Through Proverbs	Antonio Sacre	Sebastia Serra	Abrams, 2011	English with Spanish words	Proverbs	X			O		
108	Mango, Abuela, and Me	Meg Medina	Angela Dominguez	Candlewick, 2015	English with Spanish words	Fiction/family				O	X	

Picture Books

Page	Title	Author	Illustrator	Publisher/Year	Language	Genre: Subcategories	I	O	V	WC	SF	C
71	Maria Had a Little Llama/Maria tenia una llamita	Angela Dominguez	Angela Dominguez	Henry Holt, 2013	Bilingual	Nursery rhyme	O		X			
57	Marisol McDonald and the Clash Bash/Marisol McDonald y la fiesta sin igual	Monica Brown	Sara Palacios	Lee and Low Books, 2013	Bilingual	Realistic fiction	O	X				
32	Marisol McDonald Doesn't Match/Marisol McDonald no combina	Monica Brown	Sara Palacios	Lee and Low Books, 2011	Bilingual	Realistic fiction	X	O				
109	Martina the Beautiful Cockroach: A Cuban Folktale	Retold by Carmen Agra Deedy	Michael Austin	Peachtree, 2007	Bilingual	Folktale					X	O
109	Maya's Blanket/La manta de Maya	Monica Brown	David Diaz	Children's Book Press, 2015	Bilingual	Fiction/family				O	X	
33	Maybe Something Beautiful: How Art Transformed a Neighborhood	F. Isabel Campoy and Theresa Howell	Rafael López	Houghton Mifflin Harcourt, 2016	English	Realistic fiction	X		O			
110	Mice and Beans/Arroz con frijoles	Pam Muñoz Ryan	Joe Cepeda	Scholastic, 2001	English and Spanish editions	Magical realism	O			X		

Picture Books

Page	Title	Author	Illustrator	Publisher/Year	Language	Genre: Subcategories	I	O	V	WC	SF	C
90	*My Abuelita*	Tony Johnston	Yuyi Morales	HMH Books for Young Readers, 2009	English with Spanish words	Realistic fiction	O			X		
33	*My Diary from Here to There/Mi diario de aqui hasta allá*	Amada Irma Pérez	Maya Christina Gonzalez	Lee and Low Books, 2002	Bilingual	Realistic fiction	X	O				
110	*My Granny Went to Market/Abuelita fue al mercado*	Stella Blackstone	Christopher Corr	Barefoot Books, 1995	English and Spanish editions	Realistic fiction: rhyming		O			X	
111	*My Name Is Celia/Me llamo Celia: The Life of Celia Cruz*	Monica Brown	Rafael López	Luna Rising, 2004	Bilingual	Biography		O			X	
34	*My Name Is Gabito/Me llamo Gabito: The Life of Gabriel García Márquez*	Monica Brown	Raúl Colón	Luna Rising, 2007	Bilingual	Biography	X	O		O		
57	*My Tata's Remedies/Los remedios de mi tata*	Roni Capin Rivera-Ashford	Antonio Castro L.	Cinco Puntos, 2015	Bilingual	Informational	O	X				
34	*My Very Own Room/Mi propio cuartito*	Amada Irma Pérez	Maya Christina Gonzalez	Lee and Low Books, 2000	Bilingual	Realistic fiction	X		O			
35	*Napí*	Antonio Ramírez	Domi	Douglas and McIntyre, 2004	English and Spanish editions	Magical realism	X			O		

Picture Books

Page	Title	Author	Illustrator	Publisher/Year	Language	Genre: Subcategories	I	O	V	WC	SF	C
71	Niño Wrestles the World	Yuyi Morales	Yuyi Morales	Roaring Brook 2013	English with Spanish words	Fantasy			X	O		
91	The Old Man and His Door/El viejo y su puerta	Gary Soto	Joe Cepeda	G. P. Putnam's Sons, 1996	English and Spanish editions	Realistic fiction	O			X		
35	Pablo Neruda: Poet of the People	Monica Brown	Julie Paschkis	Henry Holt, 2011	English	Biography	X		O	O		
36	Pancho Rabbit and the Coyote: A Migrant's Tale	Duncan Tonatiuh	Duncan Tonatiuh	Abrams, 2013	English	Folktale	X			O		
36	Parrots Over Puerto Rico	Susan L. Roth and Cindy Trumbore	Susan L. Roth	Lee and Low Books, 2013	English	Narrative nonfiction	X		O			
72	The Rainbow Tulip	Pat Mora	Elizabeth Sayles	Puffin Books, 2003	English with Spanish words	Memoir			X	O		
111	Round Is a Tortilla	Roseanne Greenfield Thong	John Parra	Chronicle Books, 2015	English with Spanish words	Narrative nonfiction				O	X	
58	Rubia and the Three Osos	Susan Middleton Elya	Melissa Sweet	Disney-Hyperion Books, 2010	English	Fairy tale		X			O	

Picture Books

Page	Title	Author	Illustrator	Publisher/Year	Language	Genre: Subcategories	I	O	V	WC	SF	C
112	The Runaway Piggy/El cochinito fugitivo	James Luna	Laura Lacámara	Piñata Books, 2010	Bilingual	Fiction, narrative					X	O
36	Separate Is Never Equal: Sylvia Mendez and Her Family's Fight for Desegregation	Duncan Tonatiuh	Duncan Tonatiuh	Abrams, 2014	Bilingual	Biography	X		O			
91	Side by Side/Lado a lado: The Story of Dolores Huerta and Cesar Chavez/La historia de Dolores Huerta y César Chávez	Monica Brown	Joe Cepeda	Rayo, 2010	Bilingual	Biography	O			X		
92	Siesta	Ginger Foglesong Guy	René King Moreno	HarperCollins, 2005	Bilingual	Realistic fiction				X	O	
112	Sonia Sotomayor: A Judge Grows in the Bronx/La juez que creció en el Bronx	Jonah Winter	Edel Rodriguez	Atheneum Books for Young Readers, 2009	Bilingual	Biography	O				X	
37	A Spoon for Every Bite/Una cuchara para cada bocado	Joe Hayes	Rebecca Leer	Cinco Puntos, 2005	Bilingual	Folklore	X			O		

Picture Books

Page	Title	Author	Illustrator	Publisher/Year	Language	Genre: Subcategories	I	O	V	WC	SF	C
113	*Talking with Mother Earth: Poems/Hablando con madre tierra: poemas*	Jorge Argueta	Lucía Angela Pérez	Groundwood Books, 2006	Bilingual	Poetry	O				X	
58	*Tamalitos: A Cooking Poem/Un poema para cocinar*	Jorge Argueta	Domi	Groundwood Books, 2013	Bilingual	Poetry: recipes	O	X		O		
113	*Tito Puente: Mambo King/Rey del mambo*	Monica Brown	Rafael López	Rayo, 2013	Bilingual	Biography			O		X	
37	*Tomás and the Library Lady/Tomás y la señora de la biblioteca*	Pat Mora	Raúl Colón	Dragonfly Books, 1997	English and Spanish editions	Realistic fiction	X	O	O			
113	*The Upside Down Boy/ El niño de cabeza*	Juan Felipe Herrera	Elizabeth Gómez	Lee and Low Books, 2000	Bilingual	Realistic fiction	O				X	
38	*Viva Frida*	Yuyi Morales	Tim O'Meara (photographer)	Roaring Book Press, 2014	Bilingual	Biography	X			O		
59	*Waiting for the Biblioburro*	Monica Brown	John Parra	Tricycle, 2011	English with Spanish words	Realistic fiction	O	X				
92	*What Can You Do with a Paleta?/¿Qué puedes hacer con una paleta?*	Carmen Tafolla	Magaly Morales	Dragonfly Books, 2009	Bilingual	Narrative nonfiction	O			X		

Page	Title	Author	Illustrator	Publisher/Year	Language	Genre: Subcategories	I	O	V	WC	SF	C
Picture Books												
93	*The Woman Who Outshone the Sun/La muyer qui brillaba aún mas que el sol*	From a poem by Alejandro Cruz Martinez; Story by Rosalma Zubizarreta, Harriet Rohmer, and David Schecter	Fernando Olivera	Lee and Low Books, 1991	Bilingual	Folklore			O	X		
Chapter Books												
93	*90 Miles to Havana*	Enrique Flores-Galbis	n/a	Roaring Brook, 2010	English	Realistic fiction	O			X		
72	*Any Small Goodness: A Novel of the Barrio*	Tony Johnston	Raúl Colón	Scholastic, 2001	English with Spanish words	Realistic fiction	O		X	O		
59	*Baila, Nana, baila/ Dance, Nana, Dance*	Retold by Joe Hayes	Mauricio Trenard Sayago	Cinco Puntos, 2008	Bilingual	Folktale	O	X				
94	*Becoming Naomi León/ Yo, Naomi León*	Pam Muñoz Ryan	n/a	Scholastic, 2004	English and Spanish editions	Realistic fiction	O		O	X		
95	*The Color of My Words/ El color de mis palabras*	Lynn Joseph	n/a	HarperCollins, 2001	English and Spanish editions	Realistic fiction	O			X		

Page	Title	Author	Illustrator	Publisher/Year	Language	Genre: Subcategories	I	O	V	WC	SF	C
Chapter Books												
38	Dancing Home/Nacer bailando	Alma Flor Ada and Gabriel M. Zubizarreta	n/a	Atheneum, 2013	English and Spanish editions	Realistic fiction	X		O			
60	The Day It Snowed Tortillas/El día que nevaron tortillas	Joe Hayes	Antonio Castro L.	Cinco Puntos, 2003	Bilingual	Folktales	O	X				
96	The Dreamer/El soñador	Pam Muñoz Ryan Translated by Iñigo Javaloyes	Peter Sís	Scholastic, 2010	English and Spanish editions	Magical realism				X	O	
115	Enchanted Air: Two Cultures, Two Wings: A Memoir	Margarita Engle	Edel Rodriguez	Atheneum Books for Young Readers, 2015	English	Memoir/poetry	O				X	
97	Esperanza Rising/Esperanza renace	Pam Muñoz Ryan	n/a	Scholastic, 2000	English and Spanish editions	Realistic fiction				X	O	
73	The Honey Jar	Rigoberta Menchú with Dante Liano	Domi	Groundwood Books, 2006	English with Spanish words	Folktales			X	O	O	
74	The House on Mango Street/La casa en Mango Street	Sandra Cisneros	n/a	Random House, 1984	English and Spanish editions	Realistic fiction			X	O		

Page	Title	Author	Illustrator	Publisher/Year	Language	Genre: Subcategories	I	O	V	WC	SF	C
Chapter Books												
75	How Tía Lola Came to ~~Visit~~ Stay/De cómo Tía Lola vino ~~de visita~~ a quedarse	Julia Alvarez (translated by Liliana Valenzuela)	n/a	Random House Children's Books, 2001	English and Spanish editions	Realistic fiction			X	O		
39	Island Treasures	Alma Flor Ada	Antonio Martorell and Edel Rodriguez	Atheneum, 2015	English	Memoir	X			O		
114	A Kid's Guide to Latino History: More Than 50 Activities	Valerie Pertrillo	n/a	Chicago Review, 2009	English	How-to	O	O			X	
116	The Lightning Dreamer: Cuba's Greatest Abolitionist	Margarita Engle	n/a	Houghton Mifflin Harcourt, 2013	English with Spanish words	Historical fictionalized biography in verse	O				X	
97	Lowriders in Space (Book 1)	Cathy Camper	Raul the Third	Chronicle Books, 2014	English with Spanish words	Graphic novel		O	O	X		
75	My Name Is Maria Isabel/Me llamo Maria Isabel	Alma Flor Ada	K. Dyble Thompson	Atheneum, 1995	English and Spanish editions	Realistic fiction	O	O	X	O		
117	Portraits of Hispanic American Heroes	Juan Felipe Herrerra	Raúl Colón	Dial Books for Young Readers, 2014	English with Spanish words	Biography	O		O		X	

Page	Title	Author	Illustrator	Publisher/Year	Language	Genre: Subcategories	I	O	V	WC	SF	C
Chapter Books												
40	*Return to Sender/ Devolver al remitente*	Julia Alvarez (translated by Liliana Valenzuela)	n/a	Yearling, 2009	English and Spanish editions	Realistic fiction	X	O	O			
118	*The Smoking Mirror* (Garza Twins, Volume 1)	David Bowles	n/a	IFWG, 2015	English	Fantasy/action adventure			O		X	
119	*Under the Mambo Moon*	Julia Durango	Fabricio VandenBroeck	Charlesbridge, 2011	English with Spanish words	Memoir in verse				O	X	
76	*Under the Royal Palms/ Bajo las palmas reales*	Alma Flor Ada	n/a	Atheneum, 1998	English and Spanish editions	Memoir	O		X			
77	*Yes! We Are Latinos/¡Sí! Somos Latinos*	Alma Flor Ada and F. Isabel Campoy	David Díaz	Charlesbridge, 2013	English and Spanish editions	Narrative nonfiction/ poetry	O		X			

PROFESSIONAL REFERENCES CITED

Ada, Alma Flor. 2016. "Foreword: Literature in the Lives of Latino Children." Ellen Riojas Clark, Belinda Bustos Flores, Howard L. Smith, and Daniel Alejandro Gonzáles, eds. *Multicultural Literature for Latino Bilingual Children: Their Words, Their Worlds*. Lanham, MD: Rowman & Littlefield.

Allyn, Pam. 2015. "Reading Is Like Breathing In; Writing Is Like Breathing Out." International Literacy Association: Literacy Daily. July 16. Available online at https://literacyworldwide.org/blog/literacy-daily/2015/07/16/reading-is-like-breathing-in-writing-is-like-breathing-out.

Bishop, Rudine Sims. 1997. "Selecting Literature for a Multicultural Curriculum." In *Using Multiethnic Literature in the K–8 Classroom*, ed. Violet Harris, 1–20. Norwood, MA: Christopher-Gordon.

Clark, Ellen Rojas, Belinda Bustos Flores, Howard L. Smith, and Daniel Alejandro González. 2016. *Multicultural Literature for Latino Bilingual Children: Their Words, Their Worlds*. Lanham, MD: Rowman & Littlefield.

Culham, Ruth. 2014. *The Writing Thief: Using Mentor Texts to Teach the Craft of Writing*. Newark, DE: International Reading Association.

Cooperative Children's Book Center. 2014. School of Education. Madison: University of Wisconsin.

Derman-Sparks, Louise. 2013. "Guide for Selecting Anti-bias Children's Books." Available online at www.tfcbooks.org/2013-guide-anti-bias-childrens-books.

Feinstritzer, C. Emily. 2011. *Profile of Teachers in the U.S. 2011*. National Center for Educational Information. Washington, DC. Available online at www.edweek.org/media/pot2011final-blog.pdf.

Frey, Susan. 2015. "Study Says Reading Aloud to Children, More Than Talking, Builds Literacy." July 8. Available online at http://edsource.org/2015/study-says-reading-aloud-to-children-more-than-talking-builds-literacy/82045.

Gonzalez, Maya Christina. 2015. In *Multicultural Literature for Latino Bilingual Children: Their Words, Their Worlds*, ed. Ellen Riojas Clark, Belinda Bustos Flores, Howard L. Smith, and Daniel Alejandro Gonzalez. Figure 1.1, p. ii. Lanham, MD: Rowman & Littlefield.

Graham, Steve, and Dolores Perin. 2007. *Writing Next: Effective Strategies to Improve Writing of Adolescents in Middle and High Schools: A Report to Carnegie Corporation of New York*. Washington, DC: Alliance for Excellent Education. Available online at https://www.carnegie.org/media/filer_public/3c/f5/3cf58727-34f4-4140-a014-723a00ac56f7/ccny_report_2007_writing.pdf.

Hommel, Maggie. n.d. *Latino Children's Book Resources*. (Graduate student: University of Illinois at Urbana-Champaign.) Available online at http://ccbarchive.lis.illinois.edu/Projects/Additions%20on%209-20-07/CCB/CCB/mhommel2/latinoresource.htm.

Horning, Kathleen T. 2015. "Children's Books By and About People of Color Published in the United States." Available online at https://ccbc.education.wisc.edu/books/pcstats.asp.

Hughes-Hassel, Sandra, and Ernie J. Cox. 2010. "Inside Board Books: Representations of People of Color." *The Library Quarterly* 80 (3): 211–230.

International Reading Association. 2016. Children's Literature and Reading Special Interest Group. "Criteria for Selection of Notable Books for a Global Society." Available online at http://www.clrsig.org/nbgs.php.

Kennedy, Elizabeth. 2015. "Hispanic and Latino Heritage in Books for Children and Young Adults." Available online at http://childrensbooks.about.com/od/culturalhispanic/tp/hispanic_latino.htm.

Maxwell, Lesli A. 2014. "U.S. School Enrollment Hits Majority-Minority Milestone." *Education Week*, August 29. Available online at www.edweek.org/ew/articles/2014/08/20/01demographics.h34.html.

Mora, Pat. 2016. In *Multicultural Literature for Latino Bilingual Children: Their Words, Their Worlds*, ed. Ellen Riojas Clark, Belinda Bustos Flores, Howard L. Smith, and Daniel Alejandro Gonzalez. Lanham, MD: Rowman and Littlefield.

Moreillon, Judi. 2013. "Building Bridges for Cultural Understanding: Cultural Literature Collection Development and Programming." *Children and Libraries* 11(2): 35–38.

Moser, Whet. 2016. "Diversity in Children's Books Is Hard to Find—But Important." *Chicago Magazine*, June 25. Available online at www.chicagomag.com/city-life/June-2015/Diversity-in-Childrens-Books-is-Hard-to-FindBut-Important/.

Naidoo, Jamie C. 2010. *Celebrating Diverse Latino Cultures in Literature, and Literacy Every Day*. ALSC Institute. Available online at www.ala.org/alsc/sites/ala.org.alsc/files/content/confevents/institute/institutehandouts/Diversity%20Handout.pdf.

———, ed. 2011. *Celebrating Cuentos: Promoting Latino Children's Literature and Literacy in Classrooms and Libraries*. Santa Barbara, CA: ABC-CLUO.

———. 2014. *The Importance of Diversity in Library Programs and Material Collections for Children*. Available online at www.ala.org/alsc/sites/ala.org.alsc/files/content/ALSCwhitepaper_importance%20of%20diversity_with%20graphics_FINAL.pdf.

Neary, Nancy. 2014. "New Initiative Aims to Encourage Diversity in Kids' Publishing." Interview with First Book CEO Kyle Zimmer. NPR: May 18.

Pearson, P. David, and Margaret C. Gallagher. 1983. "The Instruction of Reading Comprehension." *Contemporary Educational Psychology* 8: 317–344.

Ray, Katie Wood. 1999. *Wondrous Words: Writers and Writing in the Elementary Classroom*. Urbana, IL: National Council of Teachers of English.

Smith, Frank. 1994. *Writing and the Writer*. 2nd ed. Hillsdale, NJ: Erlbaum.

Tompkins, Gail E. 2001. *Literacy for the Twenty-First Century: A Balanced Approach*. 2nd ed. Upper Saddle River, NJ: Merrill Education.

Vygotsky, Lev. 1986. *Thought and Language*. Cambridge, MA: MIT Press.

Ward, Barbara A. 2015."Celebrating Diverse Books." *Reading Today* 32(6).

DATE DUE